The Flour Peddler

Caitlin Press Inc., 8100 Alderwood Road, Halfmoon Bay, BC V0N 1Y1 www.caitlin-press.com

Text and cover design by Vici Johnstone
Edited by Andrea Routley
Printed in Canada

Caitlin Press Inc. acknowledges financial support from the Government of Canada through the Canada Book Fund and the Canada Council for the Arts, and from the Province of British Columbia through the British Columbia Arts Council and the Book Publisher's Tax Credit.

Canada Council   Conseil des Arts
for the Arts   du Canada

BRITISH COLUMBIA
ARTS COUNCIL
We acknowledge the support of the Province of British Columbia through the British Columbia Arts Council

Library and Archives Canada Cataloguing in Publication

Hergesheimer, Christopher P. (Christopher Patrick), author
    The flour peddler : a global journey into local food from Canada to South Sudan / Chris Hergesheimer, Josh Hergesheimer.

ISBN 978-1-927575-86-4 (pbk.)

    1. Alternative agriculture. 2. Sustainable agriculture. 3. Agricultural assistance, Canadian—Africa. 4. Hergesheimer, Christopher P. (Christopher Patrick). 5. Hergesheimer, Josh, 1978-. 6. Flour mills—British Columbia—Employees—Biography. 7. Flour industry. I. Hergesheimer, Josh, 1978-, author II. Title.

S494.5.A65H47 2015   338.1'6   C2015-900396-2

THE FLOUR PEDDLER

A GLOBAL JOURNEY INTO LOCAL FOOD FROM CANADA TO SOUTH SUDAN

CHRIS HERGESHEIMER
JOSH HERGESHEIMER

CAITLIN PRESS

To Mike Carr—thank you for introducing me to the concept and practice of bioregionalism, for our lively debates and discussions as great friends over the years and for your passion for the earth and its peoples. I will miss you, and I dedicate this work to you.

Contents

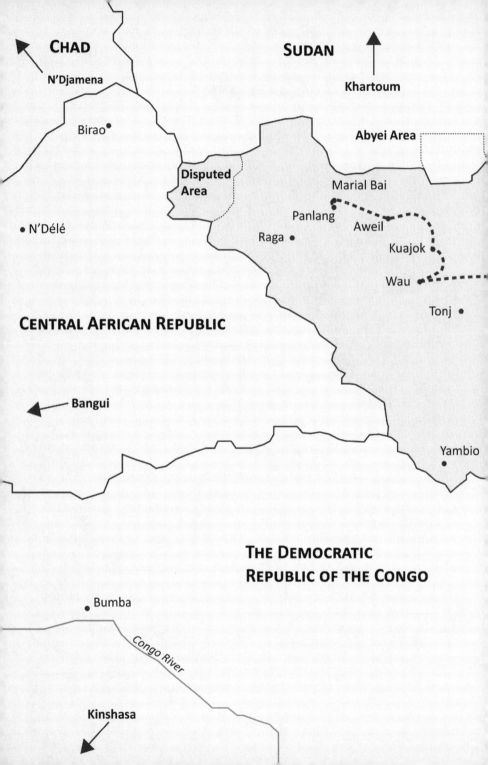

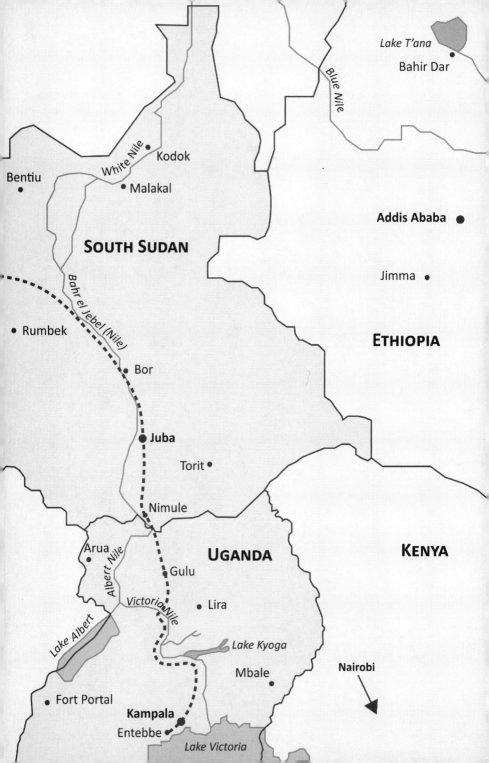

Introduction

My name is Chris Hergesheimer. But for many years, people knew me by another name: the Flour Peddler.

How did I get started? Like everyone else who does, I suppose—I knew a guy. He told me he had a special crop, grown in British Columbia's Okanagan Valley. I met the guy at the designated time and place, and I left carrying a baggie filled with wheat kernels. I went home, ground them, mixed in water and cooked it up. Just on weekends of course. Never during the week. Not at the beginning, anyway.

I've always been interested in grains, so it wasn't really a surprise. As a kid, I tucked into muffins and breads at every opportunity, and no one ever had to tell me to finish my waffles. The night I moved into my first apartment, I made a steaming stack of whole-grain pancakes, replacing the gnawing hunger with a warm, fuzzy feeling that accompanied me into a deep and contented slumber.

I can't remember how old I was when I made the switch to whole grains, but I remember the first bite like it was yesterday. We all remember our first time, right? I loved the texture of the husk and the germ and the bran, everything ground together in perfect harmony.

Chris at the village of Panlang, the final destination of the bike mill.

Eventually, I realized it wasn't just about the whole grains. It was about the freshness, about the grind. I was able to taste it— nothing stale would satisfy me—so I sought out people who could get me the fresh stuff. And then it just made sense to start grinding it myself. When you've got a grinder, well, there's nothing really stopping you anymore, is there?

I found excuses to grind everywhere: Roommates having a party? Blueberry muffins, anyone? It wasn't long before my weekend habit became a weekday addiction. Every breakfast presented an opportunity to slap freshly ground buckwheat batter on the sizzling griddle and tuck into a stack of pancakes. It was the most important meal of the day, after all.

From the outside, you'd never know anything was going on. I was a good student, having clawed my way up through the ranks of Sociology 101 at Douglas College, through 400-level courses at Simon Fraser University, and was close to finishing my bachelor's degree. I had always tried to keep my personal life separate from my academic life. But then one day, my favourite instructor took me aside and suggested I apply for a master's degree. I had a bright future as a sociologist, she told me, and she wondered if I had any topics in mind.

I told her I had a few ideas.

That's how I found out about the other grains, you see. Soon, the lines blurred. Each time I discovered a new variety, I would try it for myself to see if it really was as good as they said. First, the "intellectual" ones—the ancients, like Khorasan wheat (Kamut), one of the planet's oldest known cereal crops—that made me look cool in front of my friends. Then the "harder" ones, like red spring wheat, dense like you wouldn't believe and glorious once cracked open and ground into a fine brown powder. At some point—it's neither here nor there precisely when—I even experimented with some technically illicit varieties, like that crop of fife I scored from Vancouver Island.

It was all part of my research, I kept telling myself. By 2007, I had an official-sounding thesis title—"Weaving Chains of Grain: Exploring the Stories, Links and Boundaries of Small-scale Grain Initiatives in Southwestern British Columbia"—and a mandate to focus on the stories behind the plants and the people: the farmers, harvesters, millers, shippers, bakers, sellers and consumers who formed the food networks that stretched across (and linked together) the southwestern corner of our province. Over the next two years, I visited farms in the Fraser Valley, the North Okanagan and Vancouver Island. I knocked on doors and sat at kitchen tables, listening to people reminisce, recalling the joys of an abundant BC harvest half a century ago, lamenting the decline of grain production today, but excited to see a few fields growing here and there. Sometimes they would ask whether I, a twenty-seven-year-old sociology student, saw a future for small farmers in an age of "big agribusiness." I would always tell them I was realistic but hopeful, which was the truth. And I would always ask—as I was leaving, of course—if perhaps they had a bag of kernels, just lying around, that I could purchase? Sometimes they did, and I would load it in my van and drive home, anticipating the taste all the way.

It was only a matter of time before my friends caught on. One night I had some people stay over, and in the morning, I made them my special pancakes with freshly ground red spring wheat. I suppose you could say that I got them hooked, but it was their choice to try it. Somehow, word got out—Chris makes these amazing wholegrain flapjacks you just have to try!—and soon people I didn't even know were calling, asking if I could mill up some for them.

At first, I was worried about the idea of making money from selling it. Maybe I thought it was just a hobby or that I wasn't really a "dealer." But I needed a way to support my habit. I was already up to a few kilos a week, and when my wife and kids started getting into waffles...well, a man has to provide for his family, doesn't he?

So I set up at the farmers' market in Sechelt, a small town on BC's Sunshine Coast, offering hand-milled flour. It took eight minutes of cranking to fill a half-kilogram bag, which I sold for five dollars. I left with a sore arm and twenty-five dollars.

Even back then, I realized I had a problem. But I misdiagnosed it. I thought the problem was that I couldn't mill enough, fast enough. You do that when you're hooked, right? You deny and then you rationalize. I couldn't see that if I was willing to stand in a parking lot, cranking a hand mill like an Amish on speed while singing the praises of fresh flour, maybe the problem wasn't inefficiency. Maybe it went deeper.

Then one day, while browsing the Internet, I saw a grinder. It was designed for corn, and it was connected to a bicycle-like mechanism so that it could be pedalled instead of hand-cranked. That gave me an idea. I scoured second-hand stores until I found an exercise bike, then had a friend build me an upright wooden box open at the back with a notch cut through the top. We bolted the grain mill on, stationed the exercise bike behind the box, stretched a belt between the flywheel on the mill and the wheel of the exercise bicycle and tried it out.

It was a disaster. The belt spun too loosely because there were no teeth on either the flywheel of the mill or the wheel of the exercise bicycle to catch and hold the belt as it was spinning. And the act of pedalling made the box wobble, causing the belt to fall off. I was forever stopping to realign the box or reapply the belt, which slowed production and made the whole thing look comical. One time my wife, Amanda-Rae, walked in on me, and she didn't know whether to laugh or cry.

After a while, though, it got better. We cut holes in the box for the feet of the exercise bike so that each part stabilized the other and kept the belt taught. Trial and error revealed the exact amount of force required—not too hard, not too soft—and voila! I had a (somewhat) functioning pedal-powered grain grinder that could "bike out" a kilo of flour in six minutes, less than half the time it took by hand. It was easier to grind using my legs than my arm, and I could pedal and talk at the same time, which was perfect for a guy like me, who has something to say about most things, especially the merits of baking with freshly ground flour.

I went back to the Sechelt Farmers' Market and started grinding. I called myself the Flour Peddler, got a lot of stares and a few laughs, and left with fifty-five dollars in my pocket and a smile on my face. I had more than doubled my money, which was good. My arm wasn't sore, which was even better. But the best part was that I had engaged in a performance that had resonated with people and gotten them thinking about milling—excited, even.

This marked the beginning of a journey that would consume the next five years of my life. Along the way, I would learn valuable lessons, both about business and about people. Throughout the twists and turns, I would face challenges that would test my patience, my resolve and even my relationships. And although I couldn't have known it at the time, this bike mill would take me to the other side of the world, bringing me face to face with an old friend. But first, I needed to get this grain-grinding business spinning.

The word spread: the Flour Peddler rides a crazy contraption that mills flour right before your eyes! Soon there were plenty of people willing to come out and pay me to do it, and that made it okay, I told myself.

Besides, who had time to be introspective? Demand for my product was off the hook! At my first market, I produced eleven bags in five hours, which left me plenty of time to answer questions and engage in the banter that would ultimately sell the bag. By the third market, however, I was pedalling more than I was stationary, and I was out of breath much of the time. I realized I would need the cardiovascular strength of a triathlete to pump out the amount of product necessary to turn this from a hobby into a viable business. Unfortunately, I had the body of a sociologist—with a university-student diet to match—and I didn't even ride a bicycle that often, living at the end of a dirt road high on the slopes of Mount Elphinstone.

There was another problem. Milling is noisy, not unduly so, but enough to be grating. The plates that scrape together to crack the kernels produce a grinding sound—which is why they call it a grinder, after all—and the raspy noise antagonized neighbouring stallholders, who always seemed to be mid-sales pitch whenever I had to grind to fill an order. "Only six more minutes!" I would promise, panting for breath as the pedals spun and the flour poured out the chute into the bag. There would be exaggerated sighs of relief whenever I finished—and awkward moments when I added another handful and hopped back on, topping up the bag for a customer. It wasn't long before the market manager received complaints from vendors in my vicinity—along with a flood of compliments from customers on the Flour Peddler and his engaging performance.

It was clear: the status quo was unsustainable. From a marketing perspective, the grind-on-demand model was a success: the more I pedalled, the more people would be attracted to my stall and the more flour I would sell. But the near-constant noise I produced alienated neighbouring vendors, the very heart and soul of the farmers' market. When you sell at a farmers' market, you're not just an independent contractor; you're part of a community—a community whose members support and encourage each other. Without the vendors, it's just an empty parking lot. And I didn't want my business to profit at the expense of the community.

For a while, I was stuck. Then I realized something: it wasn't about the bike mill, really, just like it wasn't about the hand mill previously. It was about the act of being a miller, about filling the role of the grain grinder. It was an occupation thousands of years old that was drawing them in. They would stop for a look, we'd talk about the origins of grain production in BC, about the benefits of eating freshly ground flour, about taking back control of food production, and about returning to human-scale, artisan products. More often than not, they'd buy a bag.

While I was worried about changing the mode of production, the customers intuitively realized that I was the mode of production. But I was more than a producer of a product. I was also the link between growers and consumers. As a miller, I was connecting these geographically distant people through their passion for food.

I knew what needed to be done. I plugged in the Golden Grain Grinder electric mill I'd purchased on Craigslist, dropped some hard red spring kernels inside and closed the hatch. There was a whirr as the stones engaged and flour started pouring out. Just a few minutes later, I was staring at a tray filled with a kilogram of flour.

I did some calculations. If I could make ten bags an hour and sell them at five dollars a bag, I could gross two hundred dollars. There were overhead expenses, of course, like the raw grain kernels, the bags, labels, my time. But I wasn't thinking about those. Instead, I was troubled by one question: how could I ensure freshness? The flour wouldn't be made on demand, as it was with the bike mill, but it would still be the freshest grind around.

In the end, I developed a hybrid model: every half-hour, I would do a five-minute bike-mill demo, draw a crowd, then spend twenty-five minutes working the crowd to sell the bags of flour on the table—flour I'd ground in the electric mill the night before. "Ground less than twenty-four hours ago!" I would bellow, my voice like a carnival tout.

The response was overwhelming. By the end of the first season, I was moving $150 of product per market, bringing home wads of cash thick like a sponge. It was summer 2008, *The 100-Mile Diet* by Alisa Smith and J.B. MacKinnon was making waves and local food was on the tip of everyone's tongue. It wasn't just an elite phenomenon, either. Everywhere I went, ordinary people were getting in touch with their food, taking the time to research the origins, the quality, the freshness. They cared about the grower. And they cared about me, the miller.

I could barely keep up. So I asked my wife, Amanda-Rae, to help out. I would pedal and talk, she would do the cash, and we would both crack jokes. Suddenly a two-person show, the Flour Peddler was even more of a performance—husband and wife working side by side, creating a vibe that was both fresh and infectious. Crowds gathered wherever we set up, and there were lineups for our flours with people from all over the Sunshine Coast—Sechelt, Gibsons, Roberts Creek, Halfmoon Bay and even Pender Harbour. The Flour Peddler was gathering momentum.

On August 27, 2009, Amanda-Rae answered the phone, then handed me the receiver. Roberta LaQuaglia, the operations manager of the Vancouver Farmers' Market Association, was on the other end of the line. LaQuaglia had heard about the Flour Peddler. She happened to have a cancellation, and she was wondering if I'd be interested in setting up at the Harvest Festival at Trout Lake on Saturday?

I looked over at Amanda-Rae and broke out in a big smile.

This was the chance I had been waiting for, working towards, for the past year and a half. It was the next logical phase in the business, wasn't it, expanding to the city? This small-scale miller from the Roberts Creek rain forest, coming soon to the streets of Vancouver. Think of all the people I could reach! Nearly two million urbanites live on the other side of Howe Sound from me, from the sky-high downtown core and the tightly packed neighbourhoods of Commercial Drive, through to the wide avenues of Coquitlam, Surrey and out into the Fraser Valley. Urbanites, here we come, bearing freshly ground flour and a simple message: take back control of your food!

I hung up, beaming with pride, and ran to Amanda-Rae to spill the great news.

"Sorry babe, there's no way I can swing it," she said, hoisting our daughter, Gretchen, onto her hip. "But you'll do a great job without me; I know it."

I was crestfallen. In my heart, I knew she was right: there was no way we could do a city market with two kids under four years of age. At markets on the Sunshine Coast, we could bring the kids; it was small-scale, manageable. The market staff and vendors would look out for them, and in a worst-case scenario, Amanda-Rae could shuttle Solomon and Gretchen home. But commuting to the city markets would be a different story altogether. The trip into Vancouver was a huge investment of money, energy and time: a pre-dawn drive to the 6:20 a.m. ferry, more than seven hours of set-up and selling, followed by a rushed drive back to the ferry, arriving home by 7 p.m. at the earliest.

I had a brief moment of acceptance, which was quickly displaced by a sense of panic. There was no way I could do it alone. Vancouver markets attracted more than five thousand people each day, shoppers who browsed booths and filled their cloth carrier bags with farm-fresh produce and a selection of artisan products. If I was going to expand to the city, I needed help.

I dialed a familiar number, but my heart was racing.

"Josh?" I said to my brother when he picked up. "What are you doing Saturday?"

I explained the predicament. Amanda-Rae would love to come, but it was just not going to happen with toddlers in tow. The market was just a few blocks from his place...so could he help me out, just this once? I started gushing promises even before he'd acknowledged my invitation. It would be easy, I said repeatedly.

I would answer the questions and all he had to do was be my sidekick. I assured him I would pay the minimum wage, plus any leftover bags. And it would be fun.

"Sure," he answered almost immediately. "I'm in."

I knew I could count on Josh. We're brothers with a tight bond, formed over decades through our shared love of music and travel. As teenagers, we formed several bands, from punk to metal to acoustic folk, and we performed as buskers at Granville Island and on the SkyTrain. We'd also had some great adventures: a road trip in the family minivan to Yosemite Valley and a backpacking adventure to Haida Gwaii on VIA Rail and BC Ferries. The way he saw it, this was the next brotherly adventure.

I hung up the phone. "Josh is good to go," I said to Amanda-Rae.

"That's perfect," she said. "You guys will work well together." She leaned over, kissed me and turned to head to bed.

"Great," I said. "I'll have to go in the night before, on Friday, just to get Josh oriented."

She made an exaggerated frown, but then broke out laughing. "Of course," she said. "Go and orient Josh over some beers."

As Josh and I set up the booth that Saturday, I was excited, but also a bit worried. I couldn't ride on name recognition here; it was sink or swim in the turbulent waters of the urban farmers' markets. If I was to impress the market manager and get invited back, I needed to hit a home run.

"I'll let you off with a warning, this time," LaQuaglia said when she noticed I didn't have any tent weights. I'd never even heard of tent weights! But I couldn't let her think I was a country bumpkin; I had to show her I was a professional. Thankfully, before I tried to make up an excuse, she said, "Be sure that's sorted out for next time."

It was early September, and the stalls were bursting with peaches, heirloom tomatoes and squash. I was decked out in striped overalls and a straw hat; I figured that playing up the country shtick might help. The table was set up in front of our van with seventy bags of flour that had been milled the day before. I preached and demonstrated the bike mill every half-hour while Josh worked cash. Families gathered round, people smiled and took pictures. I waved my arms frantically and talked about the wheat I was milling, grown in Metchosin on Vancouver Island or Seabird Island near Agassiz, with the spelt and rye coming from Armstrong in the Okanagan Valley—"A 100 percent southwestern BC grain chain," I called it.

At 11:20 a.m., Josh caught my eye and gestured down at the wad of bills in the cash box. "We're already at three hundred dollars, bro," he mouthed. "People are loving it." I broke out in a smile. This is working—the Flour Peddler is working! I sped up, riding that bike "to beat the band," as my late grandfather used to say. It was the freshest-ground flour around, and for locavores, it was pretty close to ecstasy.

We were sold out long before the 2:00 p.m. bell sounded. As we packed up, exhausted but thrilled, I reflected on it. I was a grain-chain rock star, flashing a smile and spouting off a preachy-but-not-pretentious blend of SFU sociology and on-the-ground activism. I had arrived on the Vancouver food scene, seemingly from out of nowhere, like a beat poet hopping off a freight train and reciting his verses to a crowded San Francisco coffee house. And while I was thrilled with the reaction from customers, the collection plate did floweth over as well: there was more than four hundred dollars in the cash box. The Flour Peddler had never seen this much money before.

I began calculations and dreaming about the ten thousand dollars I could expect to gross each summer.

Yes, the possibilities were endless, as long as I could solve one nagging problem: how would I find the fifteen hours per week needed to mill grain in advance of the markets? I was a full-time postgraduate student and an endlessly exhausted parent, caring for my two-year-old son and his brand-new sister (both raised in the "elimination communication" style, a.k.a. diaper free, adding extra laundry to the daily duties). And yet somehow I was managing to show up at two or three farmers' markets each week, returning home covered in flour, with a few hundred bucks and a dozen tales from the frontlines to share with Amanda-Rae over a glass of wine.

I began to consider hiring someone.

From a business perspective, the fact that I was even considering this should have been good news. And since I was now a legitimate business person, I told myself, I should be proud that my business was growing enough to employ someone else to do the grinding.

But as a food activist and ethicist, I was worried. Did having an employee make me a "capitalist"? I reviewed the standard Marxist critique: did my ownership of the means of production automatically mean I was extracting surplus value from the proletariat? On the other hand, what could be more benevolent than a community miller spreading the economic benefits? At first, I couldn't square the circle, so I held off. But after a few particularly difficult diaper-free nights in a row, I relented. I started asking around if anyone wanted to help out.

One evening, as I was pulling on my coat for my sixteenth trip out to the grain shed, I got chatting with Jules, a new friend of mine who lived not far away. I told her I was looking for a milling assistant. She was interested but wavering, so I sweetened the deal: in addition to a meagre hourly wage, I would pour her a glass of wine for each shift.

Jules started later that evening.

In the months that followed, I would leave Jules a detailed list (scrawled in dried-out Sharpie on the back of a used grain bag) of what I needed for the weekend markets. She quickly learned how to operate the stone mill and how to label and bag the grains, which isn't rocket science, but it requires a bit of practice and a lot of patience. And she went above and beyond anything I'd ever taught her, organizing the different products systematically in transport bins (the label facing outward for ease of sales), and even providing me with an inventory list.

During the time Jules worked for me, the Flour Peddler was its most organized. She did production and I did administration, janitorial duties, marketing and sales. She was milling about fifteen hours a week, producing 150 kilograms of flour—small amounts compared to the 150 kilograms a commercial-sized mill grinds in about fifteen minutes. But hey, we were artisan, small-scale millers, right?

After three months, though, Jules moved away from the farm where she was volunteering, and the once-efficient system she had implemented began to crumble. I couldn't keep up her level of organization, and soon I was wading through piles of unfilled orders with every trip to the grain shed. I realized I was at risk of losing it all. Having worked so hard to build up a reputation at the Vancouver markets, I wasn't about to just let it go.

So I did what anyone in my situation would do: I asked my parents for help.

Mom and Dad always said they were there for me. And they had "volunteered" to help me grind a few bags a while back, I recalled. Besides, they were semi-retired, so they probably had a bit of time on their hands—say, between ten and fifteen hours a week?

Once I showed Dad how to use the mill, he got right into it; maybe it was just a masculine tool-using thing. To get Mom on board, I tapped into her passion for decorating, and soon she was cutting out labels and curling the ribbons on my special Christmas pancake mixes. Whenever I would stop in at their house en route to the farmers' market, Mom would already have a mug of coffee poured, and Dad would be gathering his pocket change to top up my cash-box float.

With Mom and Dad as part-time production crew, the enterprise was buoyant once again. Now the whole family was in. Amanda-Rae and the kids were selling up and down the Sunshine Coast, and Josh was hitting the Vancouver markets at Trout Lake and Kitsilano on my behalf. I was making occasional appearances in Coquitlam, New Westminster and Squamish. The grain was flowing out—I milled more than two thousand kilograms in 2011, a record year—and the money was flowing in. I had wads of cash in the house, and that helped me believe it was successful. But was it, really? I was selling several tonnes, but was I even turning a profit?

The honest answer: I didn't know. I figured I must have earned more than I had spent, but I couldn't be sure because I wasn't keeping any receipts. I didn't think about the overhead cost of all those kilograms of wheat kernels, bags and labels when I was holding four hundred dollars at the end of a sunny day at the market. I just kept going, with all my heart and soul. But then things started to go downhill. On April 1, 2012, BC Ferries raised their ticket prices again—an 18 percent increase from 2009, when I had started crossing the water to sell in Vancouver. Gas prices in the province also rose during that time, from about $1.10 per litre to more than $1.30 per litre. My combined costs of the gas and ferry fare for each trip had increased from about $65 to $80, but I reasoned it was still worth travelling to the Vancouver markets because I could make $450 in a day. It didn't help that worldwide wheat prices had also risen dramatically over the past few years. For a short time I was safe, as buying BC grain from the same suppliers meant I avoided the rough-and-tumble tumult of the world market. But eventually the farmers I dealt with couldn't avoid raising their prices, and the two dollars per kilogram I was paying edged closer to three dollars.

For an already meagre-profit business like mine, that necessary increase was a game changer.

Here are the cold, hard facts. I was charging six dollars for a one-kilogram bag, having grudgingly raised my prices from five dollars a bag the year before. To fill that six dollar bag, I could buy BC grain for three dollars a kilogram or buy Prairie grain for seventy to ninety cents a kilogram. That makes BC grain at least 370 percent more costly. But for me, Prairie grain was not an option, because the entire premise of the Flour Peddler was to support small southwestern BC grain farmers by purchasing and milling their small-batch grain. And once you've built a business around that philosophy, then that's just the price you must pay, I told myself.

There aren't too many grain farmers in southwestern BC, period. Fewer still are willing to invest the time and effort it takes to be certified organic. BC farmers can't compete with the Prairies on economies of scale; they have to charge what they need to cover their own costs and keep growing, which means that the raw ingredient in my business accounted for almost half of the sticker price of my bag. Factor in the actual cost of the paper bag I packed the flour in, the label, the ferry fares, the market fees and a tank of gas, and I was at four dollars a bag before I even stepped inside the grain shed. Once I added in labour costs, it was depressing: ten hours grinding, six hours at the market and four hours of transit time equalled an hourly wage somewhere between a loonie and a toonie.

It didn't make economic sense. Actually, it hadn't made economic sense for a while, but I was too stubborn to see it. It was time to kick the habit.

I'll admit it was fun while it lasted. But looking back, I realize what the Flour Peddler has really cost: hundreds of hours, thousands of dollars and nearly a relationship or two. I just couldn't stop. If people asked me to grind a bag of flour and drop it by their place,

I would do it, even if I wasn't going that direction. If a market manager in Abbotsford asked me to come, which would mean a twelve-hour trip for sales that might not even cover my costs, I would say yes. For me, it wasn't about the money—it never had been—because in my eyes, the Flour Peddler wasn't really a business. It was a passion that turned into a hunger for seeking out and cultivating grain-chain relationships.

The quest to mill and sell fresh flour led me to develop deep food-based relationships: relationships with growers, farmers' market vendors and shoppers. And as the miller, I connected these groups to each other. But the satisfaction I derived from those relationships was what pushed me to keep the business going, long after it stopped making economic sense to continue. As costs rose and sales slumped, I persevered, all because I couldn't give up those relationships.

The Flour Peddler, which had once soared like a mighty eagle, had now become an albatross around my neck, dragging me down—and my family along with it.

On March 27, 2012, I was accepted to the University of British Columbia as a PhD student in the Faculty of Land and Food Systems, and I decided it was the exit strategy I needed. A week later, I broke the news to Josh over lamb souvlaki and roasted potatoes on the patio of a Greek restaurant in New Westminster.

At first, he tried, valiantly, to talk me out of it.

"You didn't start the Flour Peddler to make money," he said, "but to remind people that grinding grain used to be human scale. You've demonstrated the importance of food security, invited people to take back control of production from agribusiness and multinational corporations and challenged the dominant assumptions about how to grow and grind grains."

I spooned a scoop of tzatziki on my rice and told him I'd heard it all before. Actually, I'd said it all before, pretty much verbatim what he was reciting back to me now. Once upon a time, that was my business pitch. But after five years, it just wasn't enough to keep me going.

"Okay," Josh said, sensing my resolve. "You're right. It's over."

There was silence. He raised a skewer of lamb off the plate, then stopped.

"How about we go out with a bang?" he said. "Return the Flour Peddler to its roots."

I didn't like the sound of this. "Returning to its roots" sounded even less profitable than my current set-up. But I let him continue.

"Let's do something memorable with this year's profits," he said. I assured him there was no such thing as "this year's profits," but asked what he had in mind.

"Well," he answered, "there's always South Sudan."

Following page: The gate of the Juba Technical School.

Part 1

1

Baby Coach

I don't think we're getting on this bus. It's impossible to count, but it feels like there are hundreds of people pushing and shoving, trying to push parcels into the bus's luggage compartment while simultaneously trying to push themselves and their other, equally large, parcels onto the bus. The ticket collector is blocking the entrance with his arm, and as people squeeze towards him, waving tickets and yelling, he pushes them back. It's a scrum worthy of a rugby team, and we're losing.

I'm about ten people back from the entrance, but since I'm in a straight line from the door, I'm at a clear disadvantage. People surge in from the sides, which isn't really fair but is pretty much what you'd expect if this many people were trying to squeeze onto one bus. Occasionally the collector grabs a ticket from an outstretched hand and pushes that person up the steep stairs into the bus, which provides me with a glimmer of optimism. Meanwhile, giant yellow plastic-wrapped packages are being loaded into open windows. God only knows what is inside. The packages are about the size of my eight-year-old son, and the grunting required to lift them suggests they are of a similar weight. Where they are supposed to go once they are inside is a mystery.

I look over to see how Josh is faring. I see he's fallen into a giant hole in the road, and is now deep in oily, muddy water. Normally

A crashed *matatu* (transport van) on the road to Panlang.

I would laugh at this, but these are unusual times. He had attempted to emulate the local boarding process, pushing in from the sides and dragging a backpack, and it appears he was having some success, at least until he fell into the hole. Why the driver decided to park here and load passengers in proximity to potholes that would swallow children and the elderly is perplexing.

It wasn't supposed to be this way. We would arrive early, knock back a Tusker beer or two, and still have time before departure. We have tickets for this bus, after all, bought earlier this afternoon. The boys who sold us the tickets from a table on the roadside had assured us that Baby Coach was the best choice.

"Is the bus safe?" I had inquired, though I realized the futility of asking for honesty.

The boys looked incredulous. They pointed to the poster at their table. It said "Baby Coach" in a large font, and below that was a gleaming bus with aerodynamic features.

"Just look at the bus, man!" They marvelled at the poster. "It is one fine bus," one offered. "The best," another added, in a tone that would reassure my mother.

"But is it safe?" I reiterated. They looked puzzled, as if the connection between the appearance of the bus on the poster and its safety record should be self-evident, even to a foreigner with minimal experience with Ugandan road transport.

This wasn't a superfluous question. Earlier that morning, Josh had done a Google search of bus companies that ply the 650-kilometre route between Kampala, Uganda, and Juba, South Sudan. We were partial to the company Kampala Coach, having received a recommendation from a sharp-looking man on the plane while it refuelled at the Kigali airport. To be fair, he had laughed first, telling us that "any sensible person would choose to travel by air." When he saw we weren't convinced, he added, "You would spend your $250 and be flying high to Juba in just a matter of hours." Then he shook his head. "Travel by road involves many dangers and inconveniences that you cannot subject yourself to. And besides, your possessions might be molested whilst on board."

"But there must be one company better than the others," Josh changed tack, appealing to the man's insider knowledge.

"If one was to rank them," he replied, "I would venture Kampala Coach is best. The drivers are the most competent, and the over-crowding has been somewhat mitigated by legislative controls."

I made a mental note about Kampala Coach. I also made a mental note that African English contains the most beautiful phraseology I have ever encountered.

"Might I interject?" The man across the aisle was almost too large for the seat, which in many places is a sign of business acumen. Although the plane's air conditioning was running, he was sweating, and I suppose he was anxious for any distraction. "I would recommend the coach line Gaagaa, in fact, more so than Kampala Coach," he said. "The facilities are superior, and their schedules are kept to with some precision."

Debate ensued. As we landed, the men agreed to disagree, but told us that we should only choose Kampala Coach or Gaagaa. So it was somewhat disconcerting when our online search for Kampala Coach returned images of a crushed bus involved in a head-on collision with a truck. The news story mentioned dead and injured passengers, and noted that local residents had looted property from the victims before police arrived.

To be balanced, Josh searched for Gaagaa Coach. It returned results including the following:

"Fatal bus accident claims six lives, including pregnant mother."

"Gaagaa buses recalled for inspection."

"Gaagaa bus licence suspended."

"Seven perish in Luweero bus accident."

Josh clicked on this last one. It showed a bus ripped open by the force of impact, the chassis crumpled and the wheel axle bent sideways. The report said the driver had fallen asleep and the bus had crashed into a parked truck. Then Josh found this one: "Gaagaa bus passengers lose millions in highway robbery."

At the musty Kampala Coach office, I peered through the Plexiglas screen and asked about a bus to Juba. Tomorrow, the lady replied, without looking up from her tattered ledger.

We crossed the road to the Gaagaa "terminal," a ramshackle loading area of crushed rocks and lean-to buildings. A decrepit bus was reversing, and some people were climbing inside, others shifting piles of possessions out of its path as it threatened to flatten them. I watched Josh ask someone in uniform about Juba. The man shook his head, and for some reason I felt better, even though that meant neither of the recommended options were available.

"Maybe we should wait until tomorrow?" I said to Josh, though I didn't really believe it. The thing was, we couldn't really afford to lose a day. We only had eleven days to complete the project, and William was already waiting for us in Juba.

We had to go—tonight.

As we left the Gaagaa yard, a man's voice cut through the din of the street. "You are going to Juba," he said, phrasing it like it wasn't a question. We slowed, and he moved in. "Tonight," he said, "Baby Coach is the only one going to that place."

He walked us across the road to the table with the boys. There were at least a dozen roadside ticket sellers clustered around the petrol station, each with their own table, ledger and cellphone. These boys had a poster and a patio umbrella, and we took this as a good omen. They high-fived us, bummed cigarettes, made a call and it was confirmed: two tickets to Juba, departing at 8:00 p.m. The tickets were produced from an official-looking pad that made triplicate copies, another sign of a trustworthy enterprise. We had seats 32 and 33—the best ones, the boys assured us. Tickets in hand, we felt satisfied, and moved on to the next task: buying a bicycle.

We descended into the bowels of a multi-storey building arranged around a wide stairwell. The motorcycle taxi driver had said this was the place, and he was right. There were thousands of bicycles here: some stood upright, intertwined as if inseparable friends; others were piled on top of each other like makeshift street barricades erected during a revolution. We wandered around, comparing brand-new bikes with the cardboard protector tubes still attached, to dusty broken wrecks that would never roll again.

We both knew that the time was now. We'd be boarding Baby Coach in a few hours—so we wandered around, trying to look uninterested while somehow positioning ourselves to buy a bike. People would approach us—a store owner, employee or simply someone with an entrepreneurial spirit—and try to sell us whatever model we were standing in front of at the time. We were cautious about explaining our mission, partly because we didn't want to come across as two inexperienced guys buying a bicycle for the first time, which might lead to overcharging, and partly because we were still uncertain about the unwieldy exchange rate: "Wait, is 240,000 Ugandan shillings eighty Canadian dollars or forty?" But mostly it was because we didn't know what we were looking for. Sure, we had a checklist: a solid frame, pedals that spin freely, no rust. But how would that checklist translate into a specific bicycle? How would we know *the* bike when we saw it?

After half an hour, we couldn't find a bicycle that stood out amongst the others. It was frustrating; we had so many choices, but so little confidence in our ability to choose wisely. We exited onto the street, the traffic honking and the crowds thronging. Josh spotted a staircase at the side of a building that led to a terrace where more bicycles were stacked. As we started up the stairs, a man's voice greeted us. "My name is Issac," he called down to us, "and I will not lead you astray." He spoke the words as if they were a passage from the Bible, which I took as divine intervention. Josh and I scanned his bicycle selection while he watched. Issac didn't hover and didn't seem pushy, so we explained our project to him and asked what he recommended.

He paused as if he was thinking hard, then slapped his thigh and stood up. "You need a very strong bicycle, with a solid frame," he said, and threaded his way between tilted handlebars, brushing past silver spokes, until he came to a blue mountain bike. "This is the bicycle for you," he said, pressing down with two hands on the bars and the seat to demonstrate its strength. Admittedly, it was a nice bike—better than my rusty bike at home, actually—but did we really need such a good one? It was probably going to be cannibalized for parts anyway.

I looked over at Josh, who was perusing other bikes, grabbing the grips and spinning the pedals. "What about this one, Issac?" Josh asked.

Issac shook his head, gesturing again to the blue mountain bike he was holding. "This is the bicycle for you."

I turned to Josh and shrugged. "Are you sure?" I said to Issac. He nodded.

We gave Issac 200,000 shillings, and he handed Josh a receipt that stipulated the sale of one blue bicycle. "Come back at 6:00 p.m." Issac told us. "At that time, the bicycle will be disassembled and packed, ready for your voyage." As we descended the stairs, we saw two young boys dart towards the shiny frame, tools in hand.

We headed back to our hostel to regroup. Josh ordered a pizza and a beer, and I dozed off on a wicker couch on the covered patio, until the first crack of thunder woke me from my shallow sleep, followed by a torrential downpour, heavy drops dancing on the tin roof and dripping into puddles on the paving-stone courtyard.

⋁

An hour later, we set out under cloudy skies through Kampala's rain-soaked streets. We had hired the driver of the hostel to transport us and our luggage to Arua Park, the city's central bus-loading area. On the way, we stopped to pick up the bicycle, which was, as Issac had promised, disassembled and packed into a woven bag tied with twine. Our driver pulled over at the petrol station where the boys had sold us the Baby Coach ticket a few hours earlier. A few of the boys we remembered were still there, but new ones had gathered—older, less friendly looking. We unloaded the luggage onto the roadside and the driver departed.

We looked down at the pyramid of luggage before us. We had two large backpacks and two small day bags—difficult, but nothing an experienced traveller couldn't handle. We also had one Mountain Equipment Co-op duffle bag filled with dollar-store items Mom and Dad had packed for the kids at our destination. We had one large cardboard box packed with two Country Living Grain Mills and an assortment of sprockets, derailleurs and chains bought from Our Community Bikes, a semi-anarchist bicycle maintenance collective in Vancouver. Josh had slipped ten tins of sardines and thirty granola bars in the spaces between, bringing the box to 51.2 pounds, which was overweight, but by a small enough margin to get us through the KLM check-in at the Seattle–Tacoma International Airport forty-two hours earlier, after which time we'd wrapped an entire roll of packing tape around the box to increase its robustness. And of course, we now had one mountain bike in a bag, the large triangular frame laid flat between the two wheels like an oversized sandwich.

Dusk fell and the light faded to black. The street vendors lit their lamps and the broken sidewalks around Arua Park crowded with people waiting for overnight buses. No one was travelling light. Josh and I stood between a staggering amount of luggage: stacks of wrought-iron railings, bags filled with bulbous fruits, sacks of charcoal, bundles of used clothes.

I began to realize the enormity of the task that lay ahead.

In a situation where everyone is jockeying for finite space, and where we are strangers who don't know the rules of engagement, we had to play to our advantage. And at this point, the only advantage we had was money, pure and simple. We could never expect to beat these people at their own game, but we still had around two hundred thousand Ugandan shillings from the money we'd changed, and we were more than willing to pay to ensure our luggage would reach its destination.

Josh stayed with the bags while I walked over to the table where the boys had sold us the ticket. "Can we pay for our luggage to Juba now?" I asked. The boys nodded, and one accompanied me across the street into a multi-storey building, through to the back, where there were towering piles of goods wrapped in plastic. He called to a man, who picked his way through parcels and came over with a clipboard. "Each luggages will cost twenty thousand shillings," the man told me, about eight US dollars each. I readily agreed, and he made up a receipt detailing the bags. I paid the boy another twenty thousand shillings for helping us.

"Good thing we got that organized," I said to Josh, relieved.

He didn't seem so sure. "There's no way all this stuff will fit onto the bus," he said with a frown.

Twenty minutes passed. More people arrived, bearing more packages, piling them against and on top of the previous ones until they reached the ceiling. Fifteen minutes later, a horn blared, and a heavy truck pulled up in front of the building. Shouts went up as the loaders set to work, heaving packages, boxes and bags over their shoulders and onto their heads, hustling them to the back of the truck and throwing them up and inside.

I watched in stunned silence. Josh looked at me. "This isn't the loading office," he said. "It's the shipping depot."

"Oh, shit," I said.

"Our luggage isn't going by bus," Josh said. "It's going by truck."

I watched the process unfold like a car crash in slow motion. More boxes passed, the loaders hustling back and forth, more yelling from inside the truck. Josh told me to wait and he walked over to investigate, returning a few minutes later.

"They said this transport truck is going to Juba, and it will follow behind our bus all the way."

My heart started beating faster. "That's okay, isn't it?" The uncertainty in my voice belied my fears. But if Josh thinks it's okay, then it's okay.

"Do you actually believe that?" he snapped, visibly annoyed. I looked down at my toes in my sandals and said nothing. "We can't let this happen," Josh said, his voice dead serious. "How long do you think it will take them to load all this stuff onto that truck? We'll probably be in Juba before this truck even leaves Kampala. And what about border delays? The Ugandan and South Sudan officials will want to unload this entire truck for a customs check. That could be days."

I can't take this pressure, I thought. I left Josh, walked towards the truck and watched the loaders. They argued about each and every item—where it would fit, how to pack it—sometimes removing the other loader's items when they disagreed about the correct placement. Meanwhile, other people were lifting their parcels directly into the truck and handing cash to the loaders, bypassing the office completely.

I tried to speak up, say something, but no words came out.

I headed back to Josh, walking like a dog with my tail between my legs. Seeing my demeanour, he said, "Don't worry, bro; I'll sort it out." He walked to the back of the truck and called to the men inside, waving the receipt. The loaders tried to placate him: "Sir, your goods will arrive shortly after the Baby Coach...yes, okay, a few days after...maybe by the weekend?" Josh was firm: "No, I want them off this truck, now...no, now...yes, I understand." After arguing for several minutes, they dug through the stacks of goods and extracted our things.

"Okay," I said, as we retreated into the stairwell of a nearby building, all seven pieces of luggage accounted for. "Now what?"

He took a deep breath. "Somehow, we have to get all of this loaded onto our bus."

"How?" I said.

"I don't know."

I glance around. It's been twenty minutes since I've seen the man who promised to load our things onto the bus if we paid him just twenty thousand shillings—per item. He was having some success fighting through the crowd at the luggage door, calling back to us, gesturing to pass him the parcels. Josh and I looked at each other and agreed; we left him with the cardboard box, the bicycle in a bag, and our last wad of Ugandan shillings. Then, we lunged for the bus door.

As I feel a bony elbow in my ribcage, I look around at the sea of struggling faces. How can all these people expect to fit on this bus? I've travelled in some rugged places in Latin America, and I know about buses filled to the rafters with market traders with bulging rice sacks and tiny Mayan mothers with gurgling babies and roosters and even a pig or two. But I've never had to battle this hard just to get on a bus I already have a ticket for.

Then, through the waving arms and jostling bodies, I see Josh being pushed up the stairs and inside. I don't know how he did it, but he's on! Energized, I redouble my efforts, pushing forward. I feel optimistic.

Suddenly the engine rumbles to life, coughing out black smoke. The driver leans on the horn and starts inching the bus forward, dragging the half-in, half-out people along, their dangling legs kicking people behind. Desperate shouts go up.

I'm beginning to think this wasn't such a good idea after all.

2

The Pitch

"Sparkling or still?" she asks with a smile. "Still," we reply, though not at the same time. She starts to glide away, then turns back. "John will be a few minutes. Please take a seat."

I look over at Josh. He's not sitting either. I walk over to the floor-to-ceiling windows and stare out at the forest of glass that is downtown Vancouver, sleek skyscrapers framed against blue water, green mountains and grey clouds. Two and a half hours ago, I left my home in rural Roberts Creek on the Sunshine Coast—a world of crashing waves, mossy rocks and wet leaves—my wheels crunching along the gravel driveway under a canopy of pine and cedar branches. It's twelve kilometres to the Langdale ferry terminal, where I parked the van and continued on foot. I sat in the waiting area for twenty-four minutes before boarding the *Queen of Coquitlam* for the forty-minute sailing to Horseshoe Bay, then speed walked (running not allowed!) to the 257 express bus to downtown. And fifty-eight minutes later, I am standing nineteen storeys above West Hastings Street, encased in an envelope of reinforced concrete and tempered glass.

Here I stand, a guy who's lucky to gross eight hundred dollars a week grinding grain in a shed, waiting to meet the founder of a financial firm that holds nearly two billion dollars in assets. An unusual turn of events indeed.

The receptionist returns with two bottles of water. I crack

mine and take a nervous sip. Perhaps it's the anticipation of presenting in a room where million-dollar deals are struck, or perhaps it's because I am acutely aware of how out of place I feel in the corporate realm. I turn and face the boardroom table: a plank of glossy hardwood flanked by twelve identical black chairs. The boardroom is a stage where enterprising members of our species cooperate and compete, as conditions dictate, investing in this, divesting in that, producing profits and spawning new enterprise, risk and reward driving innovation.

In life, there are varying definitions of success. But in the boardroom, success is defined simply: getting a yes. Convincing someone to invest in your idea. Usually the key is proving your idea is profitable or at least has the potential to be. Our proposal isn't going to be profitable, and I wonder if it is even worth proposing.

I remind myself that we have nothing to lose. If we can convince him that this project is a worthwhile investment, then great. If he turns us down, then we stay the course and stick to our current strategy, which is basically delivering bags of flour to loyal supporters once a month, putting all the money in a jar, and somehow hoping we make six thousand dollars by next December. I admit it doesn't sound like a particularly solid plan, which is why we rebranded it the "Business as (Un)usual" campaign in our Flour Peddler email newsletter. Catchy, I know—but really it's just two guys working for free so we can finance this project.

I briefly consider running through the presentation in my mind, but stop myself. Josh and I come from a long line of orators— father and grandfather were both Lutheran ministers, and sermon rehearsal was the Saturday night soundtrack at our house—so the urge to practise is tempting. I take deep breaths instead.

John Thiessen walks in. He shakes our hands, then rolls out a chair and sits down, leaning back just the right amount. He feels at home here in this climate-controlled world of tailored suits and attentive assistants that offer multiple hydration options. I am definitely not from this world; the carpet I'm standing on probably costs more than the annual rent on the cabin my family calls home, but I feel myself summoning the confidence needed to pull this off.

"So boys," he says, "give me the pitch."

I gesture to the iPad, set up in presentation mode so Thiessen can see the slideshow. I take a deep breath, Josh swipes the screen, and I begin.

Slide 1: A photo of me sitting on my bike mill at a farmers' market. The photo is titled "The Flour Peddler—novel concept, basic premise." Below it are our dates of operation (2007–2012) and typical weekly sales ($350–$500).

"I started the Flour Peddler with the motto Milled Fresh, Close to Home."

I deliver the first line with confidence, and it feels good. It was my business slogan, after all, which means I've probably said it hundreds of times in various settings, from market stalls to lecture halls to food courts in shopping malls.

"I only sold grains grown here in BC—which, right off the top, excludes the vast majority of Canadian wheat. Nothing against Saskatchewan, mind you," I add, because after all, Thiessen could be a Prairie boy. "But I started this business specifically to showcase all the amazing grain our province has to offer.

"Southern BC used to grow tens of thousands of tonnes of grain. Do you know when our biggest yields were? Between 1892 and 1900! More than a century ago, the Fraser River floodplain was a patchwork of shimmering wheat fields—and the grains growing on that patch of land that is now a strip mall in Delta or a car dealership in Surrey would have fed families for miles around.

"And not only did we have wheat growing beside the Fraser River, but we had millers, too, who turned that locally grown grain into freshly milled flour. A century ago, millers were integral to the health of their communities.

"So today, when I hop on that bike and pedal away at the market, flour dust flying everywhere, I'm teaching people that local grain was a big part of BC history. I'm reminding them it takes work—real physical labour—to grind it. And I'm showing them—quite literally—that the work I do is worthwhile, because my flour makes the tastiest flapjacks you've ever tried."

I look at Thiessen and try to read his face. Sometimes I can tell when someone is thinking about pancakes, but right now I can't be sure. Hopefully he's remembering the multigrain mix we sold him last week.

"Now this," I say, as Josh swipes to the next slide, "is what we want to do."

Slide 2: Three rows of black text on a white background. The slide reads, "Target specific locations in the developing world where we believe bike mills could make a difference in people's lives."

"At farmers' markets, the bike mill is cool, a novelty," I say. "It attracts people to our booth, gets them talking, gets them thinking about milling, pushes the idea of freshness, which then sells the bag of flour. Basically, this low-tech machine is a high-impact marketing strategy.

"But," I add, "it's not a necessity, because people here have options. They can smile at our bike mill display, then walk away from our six-dollar bag of boutique grain, drive to a supermarket and grab a bag of Rogers off the shelf. They don't need our bike mill, and they certainly don't need us, the Flour Peddler, as a business."

I look at Thiessen again. Suddenly, it's not looking good. I've definitely thrown him a curve ball, undercutting the entire premise of my business in a paragraph. Hopefully he can stick with us through the transition.

"In Vancouver," I continue, "the bike mill is a nifty gadget for a niche market product. But in many places on our planet, the only option is to mill by hand. People—women and girls, mostly—spend several hours each day pounding and grinding their families' grains.

"Josh and I have travelled to quite a few places—him in Africa and Asia, me in Latin America and the Caribbean—and we'd be interested in seeing if there's a place for a bike mill, like the one the Flour Peddler uses now, in remote areas where people grow, process and consume their own food. At least, a low-tech machine like this might provide an option, an alternative."

Okay, now he's nodding. That's better.

"And ultimately," I say, my confidence growing again, "that's been the philosophy behind the Flour Peddler from the beginning. For a Vancouver farmers' market shopper, I'm providing an alternative to Prairie grains milled months ago by an industrial-scale grinder in Ontario. The Flour Peddler is a 100 percent BC grain chain—grown in the Okanagan, freshly ground on the Sunshine Coast, brought to a Vancouver market near you."

I have to admit that I can still make it sound pretty good.

"And for subsistence farmers in the developing world," I say, "a bike mill might cut down the time and energy it takes to DIY the family's grains. But more importantly, a bike mill could provide micro-enterprise opportunities."

I pause and let the words "micro-enterprise opportunities" hang in the air. It's a buzzword, I admit—but if there's anything that will hook a business-savvy guy like Thiessen, it's the idea of people generating profits through their own labour.

"If the bike mill allows them to grind more in a shorter amount of time," I add, "they can sell the surplus, creating a small amount of income for their families.

"And now this," I say, "is where we'd like to start."

Josh swipes the screen.

Slide 3: A map of South Sudan, with the title "The World's Youngest Country."

"South Sudan was born in 2011," Josh starts in, the tag-team approach a brothers' trademark. "It's one of the most underdeveloped regions in East Africa, if not the entire continent. Landlocked, rough, rural and rugged. There are only a few hundred kilometres of paved road in a country nearly the size of France, and there are shortages of just about everything. Basically, it's one of the most challenging places on the planet to try and pull this off."

Thiessen raises his eyebrows, just slightly, which is the cue Josh is waiting for.

"So," Josh says, "you might be asking yourself, why here?" I swipe the screen and Josh flows into the next section.

Slide 4: A photo of William Kolong in front of Josh's house in East Vancouver.

"We've known William for more than a decade," Josh says. "In 1994, he came to Canada as a refugee, one of the famous 'Lost Boys.' His story is long, but the short version is that in 1985, as Sudan descended into civil war, William and thousands of other boys left their homes and walked hundreds of miles to refugee camps in Ethiopia and Kenya. Seven years later, William was sponsored and came to Canada, eventually landing a job on the maintenance crew at Metropolis mall. Our father supported William through the church where he was pastor. He began joining us for family dinners, and we became close friends. William was always thankful for the opportunities Canada offered and he wanted to give something back, so six years ago, he started a homework club in New Westminster for refugee and immigrant children.

"In 2005, William began making short trips back to Panlang, his home village. And once South Sudan became independent two years ago, he moved back permanently and started the Pan Aweil Development Agency to contribute to his own country. These days, he's busy installing water filters, irrigating fields to grow dry-season crops and building schools to educate the next generation.

"William is a bridge between two worlds. He brings the best developed-world ideas from Canada and he implements them in a way that fits the local context and respects South Sudanese culture. William is a big supporter of the bike-mill project—actually, this project was his idea—and we're confident that with him behind us, we can pull it off."

Josh nods to me. I swipe the screen and take over.

"We think South Sudan is a good place to run a pilot project," I say. "Here's why."

Slide 5: More text. The slide reads "Identified need: A) No electricity; B) Subsistence agriculture; C) Long distances to town markets to purchase/mill grains."

"The fact that a bike mill relies on human power rather than electricity is crucial," I say. "And since most rural South Sudanese are subsistence farmers and cattle herders, they are already eating 'local' by default. So if they can grind their grain in-house, well, that's an alternative that could save them time and money."

Josh swipes the screen, and I continue.

Slide 6: Two sentences. The top one reads, "This is not a charity project." Below that, the hook: "This is an investment in micro-capitalism."

"We aren't doing aid work," I say. "A bike mill isn't the answer to all of life's problems—but it might help make a small part of someone's life a bit easier. It won't make people dependent on handouts, and it won't do their work for them. It could, however, provide alternatives, and could even help someone earn a bit of income, start a small business.

"We aren't pie-in-the-sky idealists," I say, "though it might seem that way. We don't know what effect this bike mill could have. To be honest, we're not even sure if we can actually build the thing on-site like we've planned. Can we find a bicycle frame and enough scrap metal to work with? Can we find an engineer and a welder who can pull this off on short notice? There are a lot of unknowns," I say, "but the only way we'll ever know is if we try."

I stop talking, reach down and swipe the screen. Josh takes over.

Slide 7: The title reads "Pilot Project." Underneath, the place, "Panlang, South Sudan." The timeframe, "December 2013." And the cost, "$6,000."

"Today is October 18, 2012. That gives us a little over a year to come up with the plan, the prototype and, of course, the financing."

I catch myself wincing. I don't like talking about money, so I'm glad Josh agreed to take this section. Ever since I was young, I've felt like money wasn't worth as much to me as the relationships that I believed were at risk when money came between people. My friends and colleagues have no qualms about figuring their worth and pricing themselves accordingly. I, on the other hand, always undercut myself, charging what I think that other person would feel comfortable paying.

Too often, I've seen money generate conflict, and I don't like the tension it creates, especially among friends. Even the potential for conflict is enough to have me proactively chipping in extra after the bill arrives, or paying more than my share of gas because it's easier than having to confront my buddy who never seems to have his bank card with him at the moment.

When I stop and think about it, that phobia of talking about money is a big part of why the Flour Peddler suffered. I never wanted to look too closely, nitpick at the numbers or make hard decisions. I've always tried to follow my heart instead of my gut, and, believe me, I've paid dearly for that privilege.

"So, what we're hoping for is someone—someone like yourself, maybe—who could help us figure out how to make this work,"

Josh says to Thiessen. "Currently, we're selling bags of flour once a month through a home delivery service. Chris grinds the orders the night before on the Sunshine Coast, brings it across on the ferry, and I do the deliveries in and around Vancouver. And with that, we figure it's possible to sell enough bags of flour to buy us airplane tickets to East Africa.

"To cover on-the-ground expenses, we're launching a crowd-funding campaign to raise money to buy materials locally, hire local engineers and technicians to build a sturdy bike mill, then transport it to Panlang, where William has identified a women's cooperative that is interested in using it.

"We realize it will be a lot of effort, and it will only happen if both Chris and I are willing to work for free. So it's clearly not sustainable; we get that. But," Josh adds, "we are willing to do it this one time because we believe that if we can get this thing off the ground—and more importantly, prove the idea works—then we can find an investor willing to back it the next time around."

I look at Josh. We're done. I sigh in relief and wipe my palms down my pant legs.

"So, John," Josh says, after pausing for a moment. "What do you think?"

We exit the building into the rain and stand silently on the sidewalk. Cars blur past, slicing puddles and sending spray sideways along West Hastings Street, the sound of wet tires on pavement, a symphony of *zzizz* and *ziiiiizzz*.

Neither of us knows what to say. Not that we thought he would say yes, after all; we knew pitching a social justice project to an investment banker was a long shot. But we didn't count on how thoroughly we misread the situation.

"Guys," Thiessen had said when we finished. "I don't get it."

We had both remained still, unsure what to do next.

"You're onto something here with the milling," he had told us. "You probably know already, but your multigrain mix makes some of the best pancakes I've ever tasted. The way the little bubbles form around the edges—it's beautiful. And you've got the brand already. So why don't you actually try to make a go of it, properly? You know, scale up, buy a larger mill, and increase your production? Most importantly, buy the lower-cost Prairie grain. At least make it an option.

"Make it about the freshness, not geography," he had suggested. "Maybe there aren't enough people who would pay ten dollars for a bag of BC grain, but there are probably plenty who would pay six dollars for a bag of Prairie grain, as long as it was freshly ground by you, the Flour Peddler. That's a sensible business strategy."

He had no way of knowing that I'd been down this road before, too many times. Did he think I had never fantasized about shaving 60 percent of my cost price off, all those years when I couldn't get ahead? If he only knew how I had toyed over that calculation, weighing that Faustian bargain with Prairie grain in my mind.

"But changing the business model completely," he had said, "building bike mills in the developing world and giving them away—and you both working for free? I'm sorry, but I couldn't support something like this, even if I liked the idea. As a potential investor, what's the ROI? I can give you some suggestions, but I can't fund your project."

A car passes, spraying gutter water up onto my pant leg, snapping me back to the street. Josh breaks the silence. "Well, the good news," he says, "is that it didn't take Thiessen long to pinpoint the reason why you struggled to turn a profit. The bad news is that the reason why—the BC grain angle—is precisely what makes the business unique. You can't change the formula, because it would run counter to the Flour Peddler's philosophy. And you're not willing to raise your prices."

"He did say it pretty much defied the logic of capitalism," I retort.

Josh laughs to himself. "That's not a bad title for a book," he says. "*The Flour Peddler: Defying the Logic of Capitalism Since 2008.*

"That will definitely not get past an editor."

I notice it's no longer raining. Our spirits lift, and we start walking. Before I know it, we're nearing Stadium SkyTrain Station, where the bus to the Horseshoe Bay ferry terminal loads before picking up passengers along West Georgia Street.

My bus pulls up. I watch the door open, and then turn to Josh.

"It's not like he doesn't believe in social justice or in the idea of a bike mill," I say, trying to internalize my feelings of rejection. "He just doesn't understand why we would be willing to work for free to make it happen."

"Or maybe he understands, but wants to discourage that type of behaviour," Josh says, laughing. "He is in the business of making money, after all, not losing it."

I look at Josh. "We're still going to do it, right?"

"Yeah," he says. "After that, I'm more motivated than ever."

"Okay," I say conclusively, "let's do this." I reach out, and Josh clasps my hand. As we do this, the bus pulls away from the stop. "Whoa! Buddy, wait up!" I half-heartedly yell after it, but it's already gone.

"I hope that wasn't a bad omen," Josh says ominously, and then chuckles. "Come on, let's get a coffee, bro. Looks like you've got a few minutes."

An hour later, I'm half-dozing in the window seat of a bus hurtling along the Upper Levels Highway towards Horseshoe Bay, my mind drifting in and out of thought. Thiessen is completely right. For years now, I've been operating this business contrary to basic economics simply because I believe in the cause—a cause I feel is worth sacrificing for.

But investors, even those with a conscience larger than their bank account, always look at the bottom line. And that's where we can't square the circle. Even though our goals are laudable, our methods are a recipe for bankruptcy. Sure, the South Sudanese woman who pedals the future bike mill may have the chance to turn a tiny profit, but there's no chance of us creating a sustainable business building bike mills for rural communities on the other side of the planet.

And that isn't something that anyone—let alone a savvy investor like John Thiessen—would be interested in supporting, I think to myself as I fall asleep.

Nine months after our meeting, and less than thirty-six hours before our crowdfunding deadline, we received a personal check for eight hundred dollars from John Thiessen—the exact amount we needed to meet our thirty-five-hundred-dollar funding goal.

On the envelope, he had written: "Good luck in South Sudan."

3

Juba-Bound

The horn blares, startling me from sleep. Baby Coach swerves and accelerates past a truck. Another long horn from oncoming traffic, and the bus swerves back into our lane, narrowly avoiding a passenger van travelling the opposite direction, its headlights slashing past in the darkness.

I think back to the images of the crumpled bus on Josh's computer screen. Maybe this bus idea wasn't the safest option. But then again, when we planned this trip seven months ago, it was pretty much our only choice.

We had started the Flour Peddler's "Business as (Un)usual" campaign in September 2012. The idea was simple: instead of setting up at farmers' markets, we would send a monthly message to everyone on our email list asking them to place an order, which we would fill at the end of each month. September's delivery brought us $160. October's was $240. And so on.

When the March delivery rolled around, the Flour Peddler International Fund was sitting at $800. We were ecstatic. We decided to start looking at the cost of airline tickets. I had been absent-mindedly entering "Vancouver to Juba cheap flights" into Google and Expedia for weeks. But something was wrong. I couldn't find any big-name airlines flying to Juba: not British Airways, not KLM, not Lufthansa. And the searches were returning absurdly high prices, more than $3,100, and bizarre connections, like a thirteen-hour layover in Frankfurt followed by another eighteen hours in Cairo. For a guy like me who travels to Latin America and the Caribbean, accustomed to paying around $800 return, it was true sticker shock.

I was momentarily excited when I found a flight on Egypt Air from Toronto to Juba for $1,500. But once we included the cost of a return flight from Vancouver to Toronto (flying across Canada in late December was an expensive proposition), it was closer to $2,500, and I couldn't find availability on the dates we wanted.

Eventually, Josh found us a way: fly on KLM to Uganda and travel overland. He found tickets for Vancouver to Entebbe for $1,880 return. Josh assured me we could get a bus from Kampala to Juba; the going price was $40 each way, according to the Lonely Planet Thorn Tree travel forum. That combination would put us in Juba for less than $2,000 each, he said. Daunting, we decided, but doable.

Of course, landing in Uganda and going overland would add 650 kilometres to the length of the journey. The A43, Uganda's main north–south artery, is a particularly deadly stretch of road, known for aggressive driving and head-on collisions that claim hundreds of lives annually. And travelling overland meant we would have to cross the border between Uganda and South Sudan—a border with a reputation for lengthy delays and rampant corruption—carrying two grain mills and a box full of bicycle parts.

But Josh wasn't worried about those things. Actually, those were the things that sold him on the trip in the first place. Like me, he finds the struggle of this type of travel appealing, battling the rough roads and bureaucratic quagmires on the quest for the ultimate adventure. Besides, the last time he was on African soil was three years earlier in Ethiopia, and I knew he was anxious to return.

Baby Coach pulled away from the curb at 9:15 p.m. We crawled through the traffic around Arua Park, following the long line of tail lights that snaked their way over Kampala's rumpled hills. As we settled in for the estimated twelve-hour ride, Josh introduced himself to Grace, the lovely Ugandan woman with sculpted hair sitting between him and the window. Josh asked if she'd been to Juba before. She's working there, she answered. I asked her if there were many Ugandans working there. She said yes, because the pay is better. We asked her if she likes it. She didn't answer, just looked down at her phone and started texting her friends.

After twenty minutes, it felt like we were starting to break free from the traffic. Finally, we're on the move! Then the bus cranked a left into a petrol station and pulled up next to the pumps. The driver left the bus idling and the attendants opened the gas tank and began fuelling. This is not something that normally happens in Canada, but anyone who travels in the developing world will have noticed this perplexing filling technique. I've often wondered why they do this, given that it appears inefficient (burns up gas) as well as risky (could explode).

The street vendors clustered around the petrol station used the refuelling stop as an entrepreneurial opportunity. Women clambered aboard carrying plastic buckets filled with soft drinks on ice, and balancing wide basins stacked with steaming balls of corn flour on their heads, and began threading their way through the passengers and piles of possessions. A woman carrying a tub of deep-fried grasshoppers squeezed past me, then turned and gestured to us, waving the stack of paper cones she uses to serve up the insects. Josh claimed to be full from the pizza and passed, but I figured that as an adventurous sociologist and food activist, I should give it a try. I couldn't convince the vendor to sell me a single, however, and after Grace explained that there was a ten-bug minimum purchase, I declined. Instead, I turned to the window and watched the station attendants argue with the driver and conductor about how much they should fill the gas tank. Then we swung back out onto the road.

The few hours since then have been a blur. Horns honking, narrow misses, gasps for breath as the passengers cling to the seatbacks for dear life. Somehow I nod off, only to be awoken as the bus pulls to a stop next to the bright lights of a highway rest area. People start climbing off, so Josh and I follow. I check my watch: 2:18 a.m. The air is cooler now, and my shirt, which once was sticky, has dried.

As the passengers disembark, young girls approach us selling skewers of goat meat. Josh fishes some coins out of his pocket and buys six sticks. He gives two to Grace, ensuring we stay on good terms with our seatmate. Worried about the food-safe quality of the meat, I pass, even though I'm feeling quite hungry.

Josh and I join the single-file line to enter the men's bathroom. There's a paper sign taped on the porcelain wall: two hundred shillings—about ten cents. Josh checks his pockets, comes up empty. "Do you have any shillings left, bro?" he asks. I check my pockets: nothing. We had given the last of our paper money to the guy who promised to get our things on the bus. And the irony is that we still don't know if our things are even on the bus. We managed to get ourselves on, but it was too crowded to see if the box and the bicycle made it into the luggage compartment below. We just have to hope they are there when those doors open in Juba.

The line shuffles forward. Josh sighs and gets out a US one-dollar bill. The man in front of us notices the bill and turns around. "Please do not pay such an exorbitant amount for your urination only," he says.

"We have no Ugandan currency," Josh explains to the man, who shakes his head.

"These custodial workers will not provide you with the optimal exchange rate. In fact, it is unlikely they will even provide you with change. Here," the man says, after thinking for a moment, "please allow me to pay your admission to the facilities." He hands Josh two shiny silver coins. I feel strange accepting this man's generosity, since it's not like we can't afford it; we're travelling with more than three thousand US dollars in cash—thirty crisp one-hundred-dollar notes and an assortment of small bills.

Josh tries to give the man the dollar bill, but he waves it off. Josh thanks him, and then engages in conversation while we wait. "Is the bus always so busy?"

"The first bus is often busy," the man begins.

"The first?" I interject. "You mean there are two?"

The man looks at me. "Sometimes, there are two."

I look over at Josh. What does that mean?

"That is why there is such tumult for the first bus," he continues. "Because no one knows for sure if, or when, the second bus will be dispatched. Therefore, all the people who have tickets for travel on that day will try to ensure that they board the first bus, as they cannot be assured of passage on the second bus."

"But," I start in, "we bought seats on that first bus, specifically."

The man looks exasperated. "What was your ticket number?" he asks Josh, who looks at the crumpled paper in his hand and tells him we have seats 32 and 33. "No!" the man half shouts, startling the person in front of him. "That is the problem—you believe you were sold a seat. You were simply sold a ticket, two tickets in fact, numbered 32 and 33."

He looks at Josh, then at me, to see if the penny has dropped.

"If they did not inform you of this fact, they are engaging in fraudulent business practices!" he raises his voice again. "These independent ticket sellers, they just sell tickets, sometimes with scant regard for the regulations or for the consequences of their aberrant actions."

I look at Josh. I'm not sure I totally understand—is he saying that the bus was oversold, or that we were competing with another set of 32 and 33?

"So, by that logic," Josh says, trying to follow it through to its conclusion, "if we had not been able to get on this Baby Coach, then there would have been another Baby Coach, the second one, that we could have used those tickets for?"

"Maybe," the man answers. "But that one would have been very crowded."

I'm jolted awake by a loud clank. Baby Coach shudders, then sways to the side like a ship. Luggage tumbles from the overhead racks, falling onto the people sitting in the aisle. Beside me, a girl squeals, so I reach over to lift a gym bag off her shoulders and hoist it back up onto the rack. The girl is sitting on a square of cardboard on the floor, holding her younger sister in her lap.

When did they show up? I must have been asleep for a while.

I rub my eyes and turn toward Josh. He's awake, but his eyes are slits, like snake eyes. He looks envious that I dozed off. "They got on a while ago," he whispers. "I offered them your seat, but they refused and just sat on the floor."

Outside it's still dark, but to the east I can see the sky is lightening. Silhouettes slip past the window, and I can tell the landscape has changed. Before I dozed off, we were somewhere in central Uganda, enveloped by dense foliage—leafy trees pressing against the narrow roadway, creating an eerie tunnel effect. But now the terrain is wide open—gnarled trees with few leaves, scrubby bushes, dry grasses. As the sun creeps over the horizon, I can make out the triangular roofs of thatched huts in the distance, puffs of smoke from morning cooking fires.

A big dip, then a bump, and the bus leans to the right, uncomfortably close to tipping over. "This would be a bad place to break down," Josh says, as we sway back the other direction. "Look around you," he whispers. "Each row has six or seven people wedged in. There are at least fifteen rows. That's a whole lot of people who would need to cram onto the next bus."

The bus shudders as we hit a washboard section.

"Assuming there is space on the next bus," I add, just to ensure we had fully articulated the precariousness of the situation.

"At least one of us could ride the bike," Josh replies, half laughing. I give a tired grin, but inside I'm not amused.

A thud, and the axle rattles violently. The driver hits the brakes and swerves hard. I can't understand how any of these buses make it! This is just one of thousands of buses travelling right now across the African continent—overcrowded, poorly maintained, under-inspected boxes on wheels, driven by overstretched and underpaid drivers who race to their destinations, passing any competitor on the road, risking their lives and the lives of their passengers, chasing that tiny slice of profit. I grab the seat in front of me, lean my head on my wrists, and utter a prayer: please don't let Baby Coach break down out here.

"Bad news, bro." It was Josh's voice at the other end of the line. March 19, 2013, was one of those wet West Coast days when the rain blows sideways. I'd answered the call while sitting in the parking lot of the Gumboot Café in Roberts Creek. The defroster was blasting to clear the steamed-up windshield, so I couldn't hear Josh properly. I slapped the vent-control slider across and the noise cut out. Josh continued, "Chris, the price of that ticket to Uganda just went through the roof."

One thing I know about Josh is that he is a bit cheap, especially when it comes to airline tickets. A few years back, I needed to fly to Italy for the Terra Madre slow-food conference, and Josh found me a ticket for nine hundred dollars. But by the time I got around to booking it a week later, the price was nearly eleven hundred dollars. I remember getting the feeling that he was annoyed at me for not booking it sooner. I told him I hadn't had all the money at the time, which was sort of true but wasn't the real reason I hadn't made the booking. But to him, the reason didn't matter. In his mind, that two hundred dollars was completely unnecessary, an "extra" charge that I didn't need to pay. He made a big deal out of it and made me feel irresponsible. I told him it wasn't any of his business, which made things awkward between us for a while.

So this time, I was ready to tell him not to worry. I didn't want this small amount to cause us any strife. "How much are we talking here?" I asked.

A short silence, then he replied, "Almost eight hundred dollars more. Per ticket."

"Wow." I was shocked. "Really?"

"Yeah," he sighed. "I'm sorry. I really wanted to book it last week, before I left for New York. But I needed the space on my Visa card, and putting four thousand dollars on it would have exceeded my limit. Now we're in real trouble."

"Hey Josh, don't worry," I said, though I was actually worried. I couldn't let him know that. I just had to play it cool, I told myself. But how could the price go up eight hundred dollars in four days? It seemed impossible. "I totally understand, and I wouldn't have asked you to front the Flour Peddler project. Somehow, we'll figure it out."

He cursed. "It was $1,880 each, I swear, just before Saint Patrick's Day. I know because I checked the day I flew to New York. Now that same flight is coming up $2,700 each. It's like it should be a mistake, a computer glitch. But it isn't—that's the actual price now. Just think: we'll have to sell four hundred more bags of flour just to pay the price difference from what it was a few days ago! It's pissing me off."

I went quiet, zoned out, listened to the rain rapping on the roof. While we were talking, the windshield fogged up again, which made everything feel hazy and surreal. On the other end of the phone, Josh was still talking, but I wasn't listening. I was racking my brain trying to figure this out.

Josh had warned me this might happen. According to our financial projections, we figured it would take us until October to sell enough flour to buy the tickets. But we also knew that plane tickets aren't things you save up for and buy right before you go; prices rise as departure dates draw closer, which would make the tickets prohibitively expensive. We couldn't rely on a last-minute seat sale to Uganda, so we were stuck.

Recognizing the futility of the situation, Josh calculated that he could lend the Flour Peddler the money for the airline tickets once he got back from New York. He must be fuming right now, I thought, and the worst part is that he's not mad at me; he's mad at himself, which means there's nothing I can say to make things any better.

"Are there other options?" I asked, though I knew he'd already thought of that.

"Yeah, we could do Seattle to Entebbe, $1,960 US. That's like $2,100 Canadian. So I hate to say this, and I know we wanted to keep it 100 percent BC, but spending six hundred dollars more, each, just to fly from Vancouver? Sorry, but we just can't afford it. And we obviously can't wait any longer. We've got to book it. Now."

"Give me a chance to check with Amanda-Rae," I pleaded. I was stalling for time, not because I didn't want to go, but because buying the tickets meant making the commitment—and all of a sudden I got a sinking feeling, and I realized I didn't know if I even believed we could actually do this.

"Okay, let me know by tonight," he said, sounding anxious. "We've got to lock this down."

I put down my phone, pushed in the clutch and turned the key.

I threw the slider across, and hot air started blowing again, so forcefully that it startled me. As I waited for the fog to clear, my mind was racing. Could we actually do this—head off to South Sudan and build this bike mill? The idea, which had sounded so good when we dreamed it up six months ago, now filled me with dread. What if we didn't make enough money from selling bags of flour and Josh was out of pocket? Or worse, what if we scraped together enough money for the tickets, but had no money left to build the mill? What if we tried to build the mill, but it didn't work?

I rolled my window down, trying to speed up the defogging process. As I shifted the truck into gear, I exhaled deeply. Next on the list: convince Amanda-Rae.

Until now, whenever Amanda-Rae and I talked, we discussed the trip hypothetically, as if it might happen. And now here I was, heading home to tell her I needed to give Josh a "for sure" answer by the end of the night.

Just before midnight, I sent Josh a text: GOOD TO GO. Eight minutes later, he forwarded me an e-ticket in my name: Seattle to Entebbe on December 8, Entebbe to Seattle on December 21. Just twelve days. I had convinced Amanda-Rae by promising her I would get back to Kamloops in time for Christmas with her family.

We were locked in. There was no turning back.

Josh shakes me awake. "Bro, we're close."

Did I fall asleep again? I rub my eyes, stretch out the kink in my neck. It's brighter now, slanted shafts of light spilling through the windows. Outside there are clusters of huts and people walking along the roadside. Then, low-rise cinderblock buildings appear—a palette of dull greys set against brown dirt and an orange sky. We pass grimy tire repair shops, piles of gravel and broken bricks. I see the tips of several red and white radio towers in the distance.

This road, unlike the deserted stretch of an hour before, is teeming with activity; motorcycles zip past donkey carts trundling through the dust, while trucks with goods piled above the side walls, lashed down with nets and ropes, bump along the pitted road.

We pull to a stop in a dirt field ringed with fencing. Men with clipboards shout up to the drivers in trucks pulling dust-covered semi-trailers, while border patrolmen roam through the melee, brandishing guns. A man at the front of the bus stands up. "On behalf of Baby Coach," he announces, "I salute you for your endurance." I try to stifle a laugh. "Present yourselves for passport control," he says, "and we will reconvene once you have conducted all required formalities."

I turn and look at Josh. I don't want to say I can't believe we actually made it, but that's exactly how I feel.

"I can't believe we actually made it," Josh says, reaching for his camera bag.

First stop: the bathrooms. The sign on the door reads two hundred shillings. Josh sighs. While I wait in the lineup, Josh walks around until he finds a money-changer who converts a US five-dollar bill into eleven thousand Ugandan shillings. Josh hands me the bills, saying we can use the remainder if we need to get something to eat. We both use the bathrooms and emerge refreshed.

We walk towards a squat brick building where people are crowded around the door. "Immigration?" I ask a man wearing a military uniform. He gestures inside. Wise to the disadvantages of joining a line, we head for an opening in the crowd and claw our way in, where we find people separating into clumps in front of different windows. I can't see anything distinctive about any of the windows, so we shuffle to the side of one and shove our passports under the Plexiglas partition. "Ugandan only!" comes the brusque reply, and our rejected passports slide out. I throw up my hands, but Josh has already turned and is merging with the next line.

Ten minutes later we leave the building with our exit stamps. I'm not sure where we go next. Sensing our unfamiliarity, several men on motorcycles swarm us. "You, taxi!" one yells over the noise of the engines, slapping the rear passenger seat.

"Is it really so far?" I ask, sceptical of the necessity to commission motorized transport.

"Yes! So far," the man snaps back, anticipating my thoughts. "You cannot go by walking," he says, then closes the deal. "Only two thousand shillings each, and we take you fast."

I look over at Josh, give him a "what the hell" shrug, and hop on. Josh climbs on another and we start bumping along a potholed dirt road. We pass a family that is walking, carrying bundles wrapped in cloth and boxes tied with twine. They turn and watch us pass. Okay, maybe these guys were being honest about how far it is.

A few seconds later, we arrive at a small bridge. The motorcycle stops. "South Sudan," my driver says, pointing ahead.

"So take us there." I gesture at the building across the river.

"Cannot go."

Josh's driver pulls up alongside. "The border," he says, drawing an invisible line across the horizon with his finger.

I get off and look back to where we climbed on, less than one hundred metres away. "Really?" I say, slightly miffed. He gives me a "what the hell" shrug and sticks out his hand. I check to see that Josh has gotten off, then I give my driver three thousand shillings rolled up and say, "For two." He unrolls the bills and starts to complain, but we walk quickly toward the bridge, leaving him in Uganda.

The water level is low, but the banks are high and steep. I look down, hoping to spot crocodiles, but see only crushed water bottles and drying laundry. As we take our first steps on South Sudanese soil, I turn to Josh and break out in a smile. We follow the arrow on a brightly painted sign that reads Directorate of Immigration and Alien Control, where we find a building fitted with rows of moulded plastic chairs. We start toward the windows, but notice that people are actually sitting in the chairs. "There appears to be a system," Josh muses, taking a seat three rows back. As people in the front rows are summoned to the window, the remaining rows shift along. After ten minutes of moving one chair at a time, we present our passports at the window, where they are slowly thumbed through. The heavy stamp thuds down on the glossy visa page.

We're in.

As we exit the building, I realize how hungry I am. "I really need something to eat," I say to Josh, wiping the sweat from my brow.

"First," he replies, "we need to change some money." He approaches a cluster of vendors sitting on wooden boxes, settling on a teenager in a baseball hat. Josh exchanges a crisp US one-hundred-dollar bill for a stack of South Sudanese pounds, and then asks where he can buy a SIM card. Unsurprisingly, the teenager dabbles in communications as well as finance, and he pulls out a plastic case the size of a credit card. Josh buys it, cracks it open, and then realizes his GSM phone is in the cardboard box, locked under the bus.

We continue walking along the dirt road towards a cluster of sun-bleached patio umbrellas. Suddenly, I have a moment of panic. "We should find our bus first," I blurt, "so it doesn't leave without us."

Josh looks at me like I'm delusional. "I'm sure we have enough time. The bus will have to clear customs."

Suddenly, a Baby Coach roars past, kicking up dust. "I hope that wasn't our Baby Coach," I say anxiously, quickening my pace. Josh doesn't speed up, but walks towards a row of low-rise buildings where people are gathering. The Baby Coach pulls up next to a storage area filled with bags of fertilizer.

"Hmm," Josh says, "maybe that's where they do the inspection? Anyway, once they unload the bags, I can get out my phone and call William."

I'm ravenously hungry. My gaze settles on a small shop with a display of dusty stereo systems and brightly coloured jerry cans. I tell Josh I'm going to look for food and head inside, emerging five minutes later with a six-pack of stale muffins triple-wrapped in plastic film. Josh breaks off the top of one and tries to lift it to his mouth, but it crumbles and falls to the ground. I attempt to eat one leaning over the Styrofoam tray. Some local food activist I am.

Sensing my dilemma, Josh wanders over to a man who is waving a tattered square of cardboard over a wide metal tin filled with charcoal. At his side is a tray of several dozen eggs and a stack of chapattis. "How much?" Josh asks. The man points to an egg and holds up one finger, then to the chapatti, and again, one finger. "For him," Josh says, and before I have a chance to refuse, the man squirts glistening oil from a plastic bottle onto the sizzling griddle. One minute later, I hand over two South Sudanese pounds and devour the steaming fried egg and chapatti roll. Seeing how much I'm enjoying it, Josh orders one for himself.

Travel and food have always pulled Josh and me together. Though the details of specific places are sometimes fuzzy, my memories of the meals we shared are crystal clear.

It was 1999. I told Josh I was thinking of going rock climbing in Yosemite Valley. He'd just arrived home after spending four months backpacking through Central America, and he was only too willing to hit the road again. So that summer, we hopped in the family minivan and headed to California with one tent, two sleeping bags, a two-burner Coleman camp stove and four hundred dollars in US cash. Having decided to cook as many meals as we could to save money, we'd packed a twenty-pound bag of multi-grain pancake mix and the fifty-litre propane tank borrowed from Dad's barbeque.

We travelled south through Washington, Oregon and California, sometimes camping under the stars, sometimes sleeping in the van. You could never predict what would happen, except that we would eat pancakes. We ate pancakes every day. Stacks of flapjacks for breakfast, a few to snack on for later. We got so efficient at cooking that we stopped buying fast food. Instead, we'd pull over at a rest stop, fire up the stove, throw a can of chili in a pot, break out a loaf of bread—and be hurtling along the highway twenty minutes later, digesting and counting the dollars we'd saved. In fact, some of our most memorable meals on that trip were eaten in parking lots.

Eight months later, Josh got on a plane with his long-time girlfriend, Holly, and left to work in London, England, with plans to also travel around Britain, Europe, the Middle East and maybe even India, as he told me excitedly. At the airport, Josh hugged me and told me I should come for a visit, wherever they ended up living.

As fate would have it, I was able to visit them just four months later.

London was a mad blur of clattering train carriages, double-decker buses, crowded tube cars and a wild variety of cuisines. We ate Thai noodles at the Saturday market in Camden Town, Bengali curries in Brick Lane, Turkish kebabs in Green Lanes and, of course, that classic British pub grub, jacket potatoes with beans and cheese. I told Josh I wanted to visit Avebury, the largest stone circle in Europe, so off we went. The little red bus dropped us at the side of the road, where we grabbed an order of chips—French fries to us Canadians—and ate lunch among the four-thousand-year-old standing stones. As we chewed, Josh read the tourism brochure to me; it said that during the Middle Ages, residents feared the power of the stones, believing them to promote paganism and devil worship. They dug deep holes in front of the stones, pushed them over and buried them.

"This whole travel thing is pretty cool," I said as we clinked beer glasses on the lawn of the Red Lion—the only pub inside a stone circle, Josh said. By the time my plane lifted off from Heathrow airport, I was hooked. That September, when Josh went to India, I took the first of my many trips to Mexico. I spent a week living it up on the beach in Isla Mujeres, where I gorged myself on juicy pineapples, succulent mangos—and plenty of lemons in the Coronas. Later, I hit the Pacific Coast, where I ate fish tacos in Puerto Escondido and tasted real *tamales* in the old silver mining highlands. Then, while travelling through Guatemala and El Salvador, I discovered fresh corn tortillas and roadside *pupusas*. When Amanda-Rae and I visited Costa Rica and Panama, we enjoyed *patacones* and fresh seafood marinated in coconut. Then, in South America, we ate Guinea pig and *ceviche* and quinoa. Even Cuba, not known for its culinary delights, had new and tantalizing flavours to offer.

Four years after the trip to Britain, Josh and I had another opportunity to travel together. We were both engaged to be married that summer—me to the love of my life, Amanda-Rae, and Josh to his long-time (and by now very patient) girlfriend, Holly. The fiancées got talking and suggested that Josh and I take another trip, something like a brothers' bachelor party. The only stipulations from the future wives were that it had to be short (two weeks) and inexpensive (seven hundred dollars total). By now, Josh and I each had our own travel style, and so we had additional stipulations.

"We have to cook some vegetarian meals," I said. I had been vegetarian for two years, and I wasn't about to lose momentum.

"And each man must have his own tent," Josh said, repeating the wise words of two mountain climbers from the Czech Republic he'd met while travelling in Pakistan.

So in April 2003, Josh and I boarded a VIA Rail train at Vancouver's Central Station heading to Jasper, carrying backpacks filled with clothes, camping gear, a dozen packages of Uncle Ben's rice mixes and two packages of dried mango slices. Our final destination was Masset, a small community at the northern tip of Haida Gwaii, known back then as the Queen Charlotte Islands, on BC's northwestern coast.

As the train climbed higher into the Rocky Mountains, which were still dusted with snow, we wondered whether camping was a good idea. In Jasper, we disembarked into a blizzard and walked six kilometres along the slushy highway to the winter campsite, where we made a roaring fire and heated cans of beans on the stove grate like tramps during the Great Depression. During the day we would keep the fire burning and talk about the piping-hot meal we were going to eat that evening, building up the anticipation, fantasizing about the food in our bellies. To warm our spirits before the sub-zero nights, we'd fry up Ecuadorian bananas, which we'd bought at the Jasper supermarket, in generous portions of butter churned in Quebec.

Three days later, we headed west to Prince Rupert. Josh ate nothing but processed meals from the onboard train concession— glistening hot dogs in smooshed white buns, microwaved hamburgers with oozing cheese, plasticized lasagne—while I tried to make the flour tortillas, celery sticks and peanut butter I had bought in Jasper last for the two-day trip.

In Prince Rupert, we trudged through a deluge to the campsite. It rained for thirty-six hours straight, and I remember we ate a lot of tortellini, since we could boil it all in one pot, and each brother could then add their preferred sauce: meat or cream. As a treat, we walked to a shop downtown called Baker Boy, which made hot and puffy doughnuts that melted in our mouths.

It was at the next campsite in Tlell that the issue of the dried mango slices finally came to a head.

You can tell the difference between me and Josh in how we do a lot of things, but there's no better example of how our personalities differ than the way we ate dried mango slices on this trip. We had bought two packages before departure and decided it was better if we carried them separately. Each day, Josh would open his package and remove a slice, ensuring he withdrew only one, even if they were stuck together. Sometimes he would lay the slices down on a small cutting board and use his camping knife to cross-hatch cut them into little cubes, which he would then mix into his morning porridge. Other times he would savour his strip, taking little bites as he read or relaxed.

I, on the other hand, ate all my mango slices during the first night on the train.

Josh told me I would regret it. I told him that we had different personalities, and that neither way of doing things was wrong or worse than the other. He smiled and watched me cackle as I consumed my slices, one after the other, dangling them above my mouth before biting in.

Now as I watched him cut his mango slice on the cutting board, I felt annoyed. "Why don't you just eat them all, for once?" I nearly yelled. "Be spontaneous—live a little!"

He looked up. "Now I'm just doing it to bother you," he fired back, a slight smirk on his face. I turned and walked out of the campsite, heading for the beach. "I'll still have some left for the ferry!" he shouted after me.

As we neared the end of the trip, I grew tired of processed foods—and Josh. I was craving fresh vegetables—crisp kale, stir-fried tofu and bok choy, and quinoa salads. But there was nothing like that available, at least not on the budget we had.

To prepare for the sixteen-hour ferry ride to Port Hardy, Josh bought a loaf of sliced bread, a package of ham, pre-sliced cheese, mustard and a jar of mayonnaise. Every few hours, he would remove two slices of bread and start the sandwich process. I perused the ferry's cafeteria, reasoning I was close to home and could spend the last of my money, but the only vegetarian options were fries, a tossed salad in a plastic container, various yogurts, and apples and bananas shrink-wrapped onto a Styrofoam platter. It was ludicrous, I thought, trying to be food conscious in northern BC, where healthy food was expensive and fresh produce was a rare commodity.

Now, in South Sudan, I look down at the pack of shrink-wrapped muffins sitting in the dirt beside me, and the last bite of the steaming chapatti roll in my hand.

Plus ça change, plus c'est la même chose. The more things change, the more they stay the same.

The bus is still parked, so I wander around, looking for a border-town distraction. Josh approaches a man sitting at a table selling DVDs, and pays to use the man's phone to call William. I overhear snippets of the conversation: Josh tells William that we made it to South Sudan, that we are in Nimule, that if everything goes well at the border, we should be in Juba by 1:00 p.m. I check my watch: 9:40 a.m.

I poke my head inside a wooden saloon and see a warped pool table. I challenge Josh to a game. The faded cloth is ripped, the cues are warped and several balls are AWOL, but I still beat him, fair and square. He insists I celebrate my victory with a stiff drink, but I'm not in the mood for alcohol, so I swat flies while Josh sits with Grace and sips a cup of sugar with tea poured over top.

Suddenly a horn blares, and we run to Baby Coach and pile in as the engine fires up. After three hours here, everyone is anxious to get going. We ease forward and bump along the dirt road, crest a hump onto smooth pavement and then start racing along. "This tarmac is some of the country's best," Grace tells Josh, as we pick up speed. "Best and only!"

According to Josh's map, it's around two hundred kilometres

to Juba. As we round a curve, we're going fast enough to get a good breeze. At this rate, it can't be longer than a couple more hours. I somehow convince Josh that we should trade places, and I lean towards the window—a little too close to Grace, but I think she understands—and take it all in.

Three minutes later, we pull up to a checkpoint. The driver leaves the bus idling, which I take as a sign that this will be a short stop. He gets out and heads to a tin-covered shed where men wearing various uniforms sit, guns at their sides.

Ten minutes pass. The sun beats down on the roof of the bus. The skin on my arm is pressed against Grace, and sweat trickles down my back. I consider asking Josh to switch places again, but I figure we can't be delayed too much longer.

The men with guns board the bus, picking their way through piles of luggage and sprawled-out children. We hold up our passports, but they pass by without a glance. They select a few people, who get up and follow them off the bus. The driver shuts off the engine, which I take as a new sign that we will be here for a while. Josh gets up, makes his way to the front and climbs out. I follow.

We stand next to the bus, in its shadow. A soldier approaches, and we reflexively wave our passports. "Can you believe these people?" he says, gesturing inside. "Why do they not travel with authorized documentation? When I am going to a place, I would not propose to venture there without my proper identification card. But these ones make trouble for everyone."

Forty minutes later, the driver climbs aboard and we hit the road—minus several people who had disembarked with the officials. The pavement is smooth and the scenery is a blur of greens and browns: low hills, patchy trees, thatched huts, cows in scrubland, lanky kids.

At 2:14 p.m. the first high-rises come into view. It's like a mirage, these seven-storey buildings towering over the plains. As we cross a steel-girder bridge, I watch dozens of pumper trucks drawing water from the wide brown Nile River. Boys are jumping into the river, and I assure Josh I will jump in too once we get settled at our hotel. Then the bus cranks a hard left, and we bump down a rutted-out, narrow dirt lane lined with houses made from logs and metal panels. There's a hiss as the driver throws the transmission into neutral, jumps out of his seat and runs down the steps, leaving the bus running. I roll my head back and let out a low moan. Josh curses. The other passengers do not seem surprised.

Three women clamber out of their seats and down the stairs. I hear the luggage door scrape open and several thuds as heavy items are off-loaded. The luggage door slams shut. "Thank you, Jesus," Josh whispers.

Then, what sounds like an argument: woman's voice, man's voice, back and forth—now women's voices over man's voice. The bus is still idling, I'm sweltering and they're shouting. If this lasts much longer, I just might crack.

I check the time: 2:38 p.m. The boys in Kampala who sold us the Baby Coach tickets promised we would arrive in Juba for breakfast. I wanted to believe it, but Josh felt this was overly optimistic—"bullshit" was his precise word—so we had settled on looking forward to lunch. Now, I'm too exhausted to even think about dinner. All I want to do is get off this bus.

A wise man once said, "The journey is more important than the destination." But that wise man did not travel on Baby Coach. After nineteen hours on the road, everyone on this bus looks ready to pack it in, even Grace. When we met, she looked as fresh as a shampoo commercial, though we were sweating profusely after our struggle to board. Now, her once-wavy hair has flattened and her smile has been replaced by a vacant stare. As the bus idles and the voices outside grow louder, she breathes a sigh of resignation and drapes her denim jacket over her head.

Josh stands up, peels his sweat-soaked shirt from his chest, and peers out the window. I lean across the aisle towards a young man in shiny track pants and ask him what is happening.

"They are debating the price they should pay for transporting their milk," he answers. "Actually, it is not milk, but a cheese. But not like your American cheese, your blocky cheese." He pauses to search for the correct description. "A milky cheese. These Ugandan ladies, they bring this cheese to Juba to sell. It is unfortunate that each time they travel, they must go through this negotiation."

I stand up, lean over the seat in front of me and watch out the window as the performance continues. One of the women squats down, unscrews the top of a jerry can, takes a sip and then launches into a flurry of words directed at the driver.

"See, she is saying her cheese has soured," he calls over, ensuring I receive a play-by-play translation. She's going rapid-fire, and the driver looks agitated. He waves his arms and tries to interrupt, with no success. "She is saying that she will not pay the price he is asking, because we have been delayed many hours, and that her customers will not pay a good price for such a soured cheese."

I sink back into my seat. Part of me wants to empathize with this woman—a small-scale producer of an artisan product, much like the Flour Peddler—but I'm just too exhausted to care. Instead, I close my eyes and try to go to my "happy place": waves crashing on the Roberts Creek beach while seagulls soar overhead, and me, sitting on driftwood and sipping coffee from the Gumboot Café.

"Besides," he adds, "it is merely a negotiating tactic. This is not the first time she has been delayed along this route. It is part of her business strategy."

Seven minutes later, the bus driver climbs aboard, throws the bus into gear, and we lurch forward. After a few tight corners, we re-emerge onto pavement crowded with motorcycles, buses, trucks, and white Land Cruisers emblazoned with UN logos. The sidewalk buzzes with people selling curtains and mosquito nets and baby clothes. Soon we are idling in bumper-to-bumper traffic. I can't decide if this is better than the previous situation—it's so surreal, bordering on absurd—but at least we are getting closer.

I look over at Josh. "We must be heading to the bus station now," I say. Josh isn't sure. He glances around at the remaining passengers, and then turns back to me. "What if we are the only ones who want to go to the bus station?" I wave him off—it's too much to consider—and drop my head onto the seatback in front of me.

A man sitting on a suitcase in the aisle yells to the conductor, and the driver merges with the right lane and slows down, backing up traffic behind. Horns honk as Baby Coach rolls to a stop, the airbrakes hiss and the door swings open. The man stands up and tries to free his suitcase, which is partially pinned under a large roll of carpeting that other passengers are sitting on in the aisle, and it takes some time and effort to readjust. The guy in shiny track pants clucks disapprovingly as the man wrestles his suitcase off the bus. We start moving again.

A minute later, a woman yells out from the back. The conductor shakes his head. "No more stops before the terminal!" he announces, his authority now exerted. There are a few groans from the back of the bus; others exhale approvingly.

We pass a large monument where giant flags fly and soldiers stand at attention. Josh looks up from his guidebook. "If that's the John Garang memorial, then we are actually pretty close." The bus cranks a hard left, and we enter a packed-dirt yard full of buses. As we roll to a stop, people start swarming the luggage compartment, porters calling towards passengers hanging out the open windows. I scan the crowd for a familiar face, but see only chaos. I pull my head back inside, turn to Josh and say, "What if he isn't here?"

My mind races. It's been eight hours since Josh called William and told him we would arrive at 1:00 p.m. It's now well past

3:00 p.m. But then, through the crowd, I see him—his broad smile the best welcoming present I could have imagined.

"Welcome to Juba," William says as he greets us at the door, arms wide open.

Page 80: Today, nearly 90 percent of wheat consumed in Canada is grown on the Prairies, but in the late nineteenth century, southwestern BC shimmered with fields of grain.

Part II

4

A Story of Grain

My story begins a long time ago. Back before you could buy bread in a grocery store. Back before there were grocery stores. This story begins in a place called Mesopotamia, which is an old name for the place we now call the Middle East. The Middle East is pretty far away, but it's a really important place, because that's where this story begins.

This is how I start the story of grain when I'm talking to school kids. And right now, that's exactly what I'm doing. It's April 2011, and I'm set up inside the gymnasium at Charles Dickens Elementary School in Vancouver, with about a hundred fidgeting children sitting on the floor in front of me. I've been invited by Barb Finley, organizer of Project Chef, an organization set up to teach children how to make healthy food choices. I'm standing behind a long table where my props are laid out from left to right: a bouquet of grain sheaves, a clear jar filled with grain kernels, and my trusty Country Living hand grinder, the one with the big grey flywheel and the wooden handle jutting out the side. And behind me, I've got a very big—and very secret!—something, hidden under a king-sized bed sheet.

The kids can't see what the thing is, because I draped the sheet over it before they filed into the gymnasium; I need that element of surprise. If there's one thing I've learned from doing this grain gig at schools, it's that no kid is going to sit and listen to you talk about something for very long, unless there is something in it for them. And there's no way an entire gymnasium full of kids is going to sit quietly while you ramble on about grain sheaves and the global food trade and that kind of stuff, unless that something is a surprise like this thing behind me. Of course, since you know my story, you probably already know what is under the sheet.

Five minutes ago, the din was near deafening. The noise level rose as more and more kids filed in: grade fours at the back, grade threes in front of them, grade twos in front of them, and so on, shuffling along, sitting down, and striking up conversations with the kids beside them, or in front of, or behind. A few kids notice the something hidden under the sheet. They point at it, pull on their friends' arms, ask, "What do you think that thing is?" The kindergarten class settles in the front row, just a few feet from me, fidgeting five-year-olds bursting with energy and blessed with short attention spans. With all these kids corralled in one big room with hard floors, walls and ceilings, it's loud. The room is a giant echo chamber, where little voices bounce around and magnify, producing a kid cacophony that seems impossible for any mere mortal to silence.

The principal stands at the front and raises her index finger. The keen kids raise theirs in response, and it catches on, spreads like a rumour. "Raise one finger if you can see me." The principal's voice projects to the back, the decibel levels dropping in response. Then she raises her middle finger so the two fingers are standing together. "And raise two fingers if you can hear me."

The last remnants of the noise die down.

"Today, we have a very special guest," the principal says. "Someone who is going to show us some interesting things about food and farming. His name is Chris." She turns toward me and speaks on behalf of the school. "Chris, we are really looking forward to hearing what you have to say."

I smile and nod. "Thank you," I say, as she turns to walk to the side of the room. "You'll certainly be hearing something; that's for sure." I laugh, but she doesn't get the joke. They rarely do, though it's obvious once I start grinding.

I scan the sea of crossed legs, bumping knees and curious faces. Then I launch in.

"You're probably wondering what this thing is behind me," I say, trying to project my voice to the very back of the room. "Well, it's a surprise. I'm not going to show it to you yet, because it's not the right time. But I will tell you right now that it does something pretty cool. And," I add, "it makes a really loud noise."

Their ears perk up. The idea of a surprise that's really loud is usually sufficient to pique kids' interest. The principal looks like this is news to her.

"This isn't going to be a presentation," I say to the kids, "so I'm not going to talk a lot. It's going to be a demonstration, which means you get to participate, and I'm going to need your help later. But first, you have to listen to some of my story."

And with that, I take them back more than ten thousand years in a heartbeat.

"A long time ago, people were nomadic, which means they moved around from place to place looking for food. They hunted animals and gathered things that grew, like berries and roots and seeds. One day they found a grass—a really tall grass—that had seeds at the top, all wrapped up in a covering. A grass like this." I reach down and lift up my bouquet of grain sheaves, the long stems standing tall, the pale rigid covering, the beard sticking out like bug antennae. The kids say "Ah" and "Wow," even the ones at the back that can't see it very well. "The people would shake this grass," I explain, "so the seeds would fall out, and they could collect them. I'm not going to shake this one; it would go all over the floor and be too hard to pick up, but hopefully you get the idea."

I put down the wheat bouquet and raise the clear jar filled

with seeds. "Now, one name for these wheat seeds is kernels. That's what I have in this jar. We also call them wheat berries because they are like a berry—yes, like a strawberry; that's right. Anyway, the people would shake this," I raise the wheat bouquet again, "and collect the kernels that fell out." I pour a handful of kernels into my palm and hold my hand open. Once again, the kids at the back can't see much, but they still give the requisite oohs and aahs.

"Then do you know what they did? It took a long time, and a lot of trying new things, but somehow people figured out that if you smashed up the kernels, you could mix in some water and you could spread that paste out onto hot rocks and cook it. And that was the world's first pancake. Who likes pancakes?" There is an enthusiastic show of hands. "Me too."

I recall the multigrain mix I had for breakfast, which brings a smile to my face.

"Okay, now can anyone guess how they crushed those seeds? That's right; they used stones—the biggest and the flattest stones they could find. They put their seeds between stones and moved the top stone around so it crushed the seeds into a powder. Does anyone know what it is called when you grind up grains like this? That's right; it's called milling. And that's what I'm going to do, right now."

In one smooth motion, I pour the seeds from my hand into the top of the Country Living mill, grab the handle and start cranking away. *Graaw, graaw, graaw,* it scrapes and grinds, the noise echoing around the gymnasium as I ratchet up the tempo, cranking faster and faster, the kids' voices bouncing and rising in response. Usually by this point I don't look over at the principal.

Then suddenly, I let go, and the flywheel keeps spinning, slower and slower, the grinding winding down, until finally it stops. The kids suck in their breath, anticipating what loud noises might come next.

"That was pretty fun, hey? I like to do that at the beginning, to get you excited. But now, before I do any more milling, let me tell you a little more of my story."

The thing with kids, you see, is that you really have to get to the point. Kids don't want to hear a lot of talking, especially from grown-ups; they want short, sweet, and back to the action. So I keep it simple and keep it moving.

"Remember we said grain kernels are seeds. And seeds are how the grain plant starts, which makes them the most important thing. So maybe someone can tell me: what does a seed need to grow? That's right; it needs dirt—what we call soil. What else? It needs water. Anything else? Yes, it needs light.

"Well, the great thing about nature is that it gives people all these things for free. The dirt, the water and the light. How do we get light for free? That's right, the sun. When I came to your school today, I saw that it was sunny outside. Sunshine makes me happy. And sunshine makes seeds happy too, because it helps them grow into plants. And we like that because we can turn those plants into food.

"Now, how do we get water for free? Yes, from the rain. For us, we get rain a lot. But that place called Mesopotamia, where those people lived a long time ago, is a very dry place. Yes, almost like a desert. And yes? That's right; you can also get water from a river. You kids sure are smart! Actually, they had two rivers in this hot, dry place. But we're getting a bit ahead of the story, so let's slow down, okay?

"Anyway, the people discovered that if they took the seeds they had found and planted them in soil and waited for it to rain, the really tall grasses with the seeds at the top would grow. And that was a great idea, because now they could get the seeds from the grasses right there instead of moving around all the time.

"Do you know what they invented? That's right! They invented farming."

When I'm talking to kids, I don't spend too much time delving into the rise of agriculture in the Fertile Crescent and the social stratification that followed as agriculture spread across Europe and Asia. I keep it simple. I tell them that grain spread across the globe, sprouting up wherever it found good growing conditions: enough (spring) rain to nurture the seeds and hot summers to mature the growing stalks to perfection. I tell them that whenever people moved to a new place, they brought their seeds along, to see if they could grow grains and make the breads and pancakes they liked so much. And I explain that this is how grain seeds ended up here in British Columbia.

The reality, of course, is much more complicated, fraught with conflicting discourses about the impacts of European migration and expansion across the North American continent, colonial settlement patterns disrupting indigenous ways of life and displacing First Nations populations from fertile land. Once the dominance of British, French and American settlement was established, land was cleared and crops were sown. And by the end of the nineteenth century, there were shimmering fields of wheat stretching clear across Canada, from sea to shining sea, from eastern Halifax to southwestern British Columbia, where there were fields in Chilliwack, in the Okanagan and on Vancouver Island.

By the turn of the twentieth century, however, things were changing. The Prairies were in the midst of a wheat boom, driven by advances in agricultural technology—bigger seed drills, larger combines and mechanical threshers—that increased yields and drove down labour costs. And once the last spike was driven into the Canadian Pacific Railway, Prairie grain started rolling clear across the country. As Prairie production increased and the transcontinental railway made shipping more competitive, grain production in BC began to flag. Even the dust-bowl depression of the 1930s, which hit the Prairies like a ton of bricks, wasn't enough to stop the juggernaut. The transformation was nearly wholesale. Grain in southwestern BC, once a staple in the 1890s, provided less than 0.05 percent of the regional farm receipts in 2001, according to the BC Ministry of Agriculture and Lands. Prairie grains had won over the rest of the country.

"A lot of the grain we eat today is grown in the provinces of Saskatchewan and Manitoba," I tell the kids. "Does anyone know what part of Canada that is? Yes, it's in the Prairies, which is pretty much in the middle of Canada. It's big, wide and flat. If you've ever travelled across the country, you'll know there are a lot of wheat fields there."

I pour more kernels into my hand. "Now I want to tell you the story of these kernels. These kernels are very special because I didn't get them from Saskatchewan. I got them not too far away in a place called Agassiz, which is close to Chilliwack. Has anyone ever been to Chilliwack? I don't know if it's still there, but when I was a kid, there was a big dinosaur theme park out there."

I know very well the place I'm speaking about is still in operation (it was called Flintstone Village when I was young), but I like to let the kids think they know something I don't know. There are shouts of "Yeah, Dinotown. I know that place!"

It was mid-December 2006. I was just passing Dinotown in my van, heading to Chilliwack to research grain production in southwestern BC. It was my first assignment from FarmFolk CityFolk, a non-profit society that has spent the last two decades working to cultivate a local, sustainable food system. Dr. Mike Carr, a bioregionalism expert who taught several of my sociology courses at Simon Fraser University, had introduced me to FarmFolk CityFolk.

Driving east along Highway 1 from Vancouver, it's easy to forget how important the Fraser River was for the small farmers who settled along its banks more than 150 years ago. What were once large areas of grain production have been shifted to hundreds of hectares of corn, blueberries and dairy operations. Crossing the Port Mann Bridge and droning through big-box outlets, one-stop shops and Lego-block condos in Surrey, Langley and Aldergrove, it's apparent how our car-centric culture has shifted our focus and threatened our local food production capacity—turning a flood-plain into strip malls.

Only once you leave behind Abbotsford's sprawl can you see the farms clearly. As the highway skirts Sumas Mountain and crosses the Vedder Canal, evidence of the river's life-giving bounty lies all around you. And by the time you reach Chilliwack, the river is a mighty force that draws everything towards it. For more than a century and a half, farmers along the Fraser River have relied on the seasonal rising and flooding to feed their fields and water their animals.

Winter arrived early that year, and I was bundled up against the blasts of frozen air. I parked the van and walked briskly to the Chilliwack Museum and Archives on Spadina Avenue and shut the door against the wind. I asked the receptionist for a copy of a report to the Ministry of Agriculture.

"For what year, son?" she said.

"Um, 1892."

"Ninety-two, you say?" she started digging through some files.

"Yes, eighteen hundred and ninety-two," I said again, figuring if I enunciated clearly, she would realize. She lowered her glass-es and looked at me over the frames, as ladies who work in records offices and wear glasses sometimes do.

Eventually, she returned with an ancient-looking tome. I cracked it open and started reading.

Through my research with FarmFolk CityFolk, I discovered

that in 1892, the district of Chilliwack reported producing fifteen hundred tonnes of grains, sorghum and other cereals. I also found mention of a newspaper called the *Mainland Guardian*, a broadsheet published in the 1840s that reported farmers growing forty to fifty bushels of wheat per acre between the townsite of New Westminster and the mouth of the Fraser River—an area that today is characterized by business parks, junkyards and car lots. Delta, another Vancouver suburb (the clue is in the name), is reputed to have produced more than six thousand tonnes of combined cereal crops annually. Today, it is doubtful that Delta produces six thousand tonnes for human consumption, though the big-box stores that dominate its strip malls have plenty of Canadian grain in consistent quantities for sale: grown in the Prairies, quite possibly shipped east to Ontario or Quebec to be milled, then shipped back across the country to line the shelves.

The story of grain in Canada is a story of cross-continental proportions. Nearly 90 percent of the wheat consumed in Canada is grown in the Prairies. And nearly half of our country's largest mills are clustered in one of two provinces: Ontario or Quebec.

Producing and processing have been geographically separated, sometimes by thousands of kilometres, and this has led to the separation of growers from millers, and millers from consumers.

The Canadian National Millers Association reports that Canadians consume more than seventy kilograms of wheat and other grains per person per year. According to the Grain Producers Association of Canada, in 2013 Canadian mills ground 3.5 million tonnes of wheat, oats and barley. So whether you eat expensive artisan sourdoughs or cheap white hamburger buns, you're celebrating the bounty of Canada.

And it's not only Canadians that eat Prairie-grown and Ontario-milled grains. The efficient cultivation and transport of grain from farm to mill to port has made Canada a powerhouse on the global cereal stage. Canada is doing its part to satiate the global hunger for grain, exporting an average of eighteen million tonnes of wheat, oats and barley annually, according to the Canadian Grain Commission. Today, grain is one of the planet's most-traded commodities: the Food and Agriculture Organization of the United Nations estimates that a record 350 million tonnes of grain was moved in 2014. In *The Economics of World Wheat Markets*, J.M. Antle and V.H. Smith describe how the world's total cereal production doubled in the last forty years of the twentieth century and is expected to double again by 2050 in order to feed the planet's burgeoning population.

It's all part of the process of globalization—of food on the move.

The Worldwatch Institute reported in 2013 that more than two million tonnes of food crisscross our planet each day; a complex web of shipping, trucking and rail routes connect farmer to consumer via any number of stops along the way. According to the World Trade Organization's 2012 statistics on international trade, the global food trade is estimated to be worth $1,356 billion annually—the global grain trade alone is worth $315 billion—which means there is big money to be made moving food between farm and table, from processing plant to plate.

The movement of food is not unprecedented, but what has changed is the speed and scale. The indulgence in global food is no longer an elite phenomenon. Two thousand years ago, Roman nobility drank Greek wine, ate Tunisian olives and cooked with Indian spices, but the average citizen of the empire subsisted on a coarse bread made from locally grown barley. Throughout the Middle Ages, Arab traders tightly controlled the flow of cinnamon to Europe, until the seafaring Portuguese found some in Ceylon and promptly invaded, in order to secure a supply for their high-end markets. Hernán Cortés brought cocoa back to Spain in 1528, and by the early 1600s, wealthy Europeans couldn't get enough of hot chocolate. Today we feast at a planetary smorgasbord of unimaginable proportions. As British journalist Rose George describes in her book, *Ninety Percent of Everything*, a single freighter can set sail with enough bananas on board for each person in the United States, Canada and Mexico. Hundreds of trucks log thousands of kilometres each day delivering Florida orange juice to Seattle and Idaho potatoes to Miami. Canadian rail companies haul more than one million tonnes of Prairie grain each week—enough to pile higher than the pyramids of Giza.

The scale and efficiency of today's transport networks, coupled with technological and scientific advancements in refrigeration and preservation, allows the global supply chain—when humming smoothly—to deliver just-ripening goods at an unbelievably low cost, which is why we can afford to eat Ecuadorian bananas and Philippino mangos while camping in the Rocky Mountains.

But because the underlying premise is lowest cost rather than geographic proximity, it is only too easy to find egregious examples of waste. In a 2008 *New York Times* article, "Environmental Cost of Shipping Groceries Around the World," Elizabeth Rosenthal describes how codfish caught off the Norwegian coast are taken ashore, packed in boxes and shipped to China to be filleted, then shipped back to Norway for sale; and how Argentinian lemons fill supermarkets in Spain as local lemons spoil.

We live in the age of the "3,000-mile Caesar salad," according to James Kunstler, an academic and critic of industrial-scale food production. And the fuel for the engine of the global food trade is, of course, cheap oil. Burning fossil fuels to float a massive freighter from Singapore to San Francisco to feed our culinary fantasies might make economic sense, as long as the costs of extraction and pollution are externalized, but it somehow defies logic.

It was this recognition of the absurdity of the global food

trade and their quest to reconnect with "the local" that led Alisa Smith and J.B. MacKinnon to write *The 100-Mile Diet*. Shining a spotlight on small farmers and food producers on Vancouver Island and throughout the Fraser Valley, their book celebrated the cornucopia growing outside our door and spawned a local food revolution. But as Smith and MacKinnon discovered while writing their book, it is one thing to find 100-mile carrots, tomatoes, lettuce, eggs and poultry. It is quite another to find a farm within one hundred miles of Vancouver growing local grain.

Ironically, it took a critique of the global food trade for British Columbians to focus our attention on the fact that we'd lost touch with our local grain. For almost half a century, nearly everyone in this province ate grain grown in the Prairies, and hardly anyone seemed to know—or care—that there had once been a moderate amount of grain production in the Fraser Valley and the Okanagan. I searched records, but the critiques were few and far between, confined to academics like Margaret Ormsby and purists. The mainstream seemed unaware of the loss.

But after *The 100-Mile Diet*, locavores discovered, to their dismay, that there were almost no 100-mile grain products. The only grain Smith and MacKinnon found within this radius from their Vancouver apartment was Highland House Farm, a four-acre farm, mill and bakery in Saanich on Vancouver Island. Of course, there was plenty of grain growing in the Peace River Valley in northeastern BC—but at more than one thousand kilometres away, it could hardly be considered local enough.

The physical hunger highlighted what until then had been a theoretical problem: until you actually tried to live the 100-mile diet, it didn't matter to you that your grain might be grown in the Prairies and ground in Ontario. But when faced with the possibility of going a year without a loaf of bread, a tray of muffins, a plate of pasta or a bowl of breakfast cereal, with only potatoes to meet your carbohydrate needs...well, you get the idea, and soon everyone was on the hunt for the elusive product.

The summer following my research trip to the archives in Chilliwack, I received an email from someone connected with Anita's Organic Mill who told me about Cedar Isle Farm in Agassiz, just across the Fraser River from Chilliwack. I had found it: golden grain, less than one hundred miles from my front door.

Just minutes after turning off Highway 1 in Agassiz onto Seabird Island, I saw the wheat fields, illuminated by a shaft of sunlight—a wash of gold, yellow and brown. The wind rustled through the oats, and behind, cattle roamed against a backdrop of green mountains.

At the mailbox, I turned up the driveway and followed the tire tracks to the farmhouse. Jim Grieshaber-Otto was waiting on the front porch, hat on, wearing jeans and gumboots. We shook hands, exchanged pleasantries and discussed the drive out and my need to get up early for the ferry. I assured him it was all worthwhile. He turned and started walking down the gravel path.

I followed Jim past a grove of dwarf apple trees—the aspiring orchard, he called it, and laughed. The raised garden bed burst with stalks of Swiss chard and small trees of kale. Jim's kids watched me from the top of the slide. I smiled as I passed their swing set, then the chicken coop, with its warm sounds of clucking and rustling wood chips, and made my way to the back of the yard, where I saw two woven plastic bags tied with orange twine. "The first soft white wheat you're going to find around here," Jim said. "It was a bit rainy in the spring, but this stuff still grew strong."

I dipped my hand into the bag and pulled some up, letting a few kernels fall through my fingers, as I felt a "true" miller would do before making a purchase. Even though it was exactly what I had been looking for, I was hesitant. I had never even seen that much wheat before. Could I actually mill it and sell it? Would anyone buy it? Did I need a licence?

I reminded myself that this was a real discovery. Like the prospector who uncovered that first gold nugget, or the explorer slashing his way through the jungle to the headwaters of a river, I had found the "source."

I had to seize it.

It turned out to be the best decision—and the one that would ultimately propel the Flour Peddler to dizzying heights, far beyond my wildest expectations. As urban locavores clamoured for any and all local food they could get their hands on, I realized I was riding on the coattails of a local explosion.

Whether motivated by gloomy reports about food self-reliance shortcomings, dour warnings about environmental degradation and climate change, or a growing awareness of the concept of "food miles," the local food movement was underway.

But the benefits of local go beyond concerns about food miles or climate change. In a 2008 article "Farmers' Markets and the 'Good Food' Value Chain: A Preliminary Study," which appeared in *Local Environment*, David Connell, John Smithers and Alun Joseph explain that a large part of the move towards local food is the drive to create what has been termed a "good food value chain," one which "conveys the notion that activities within the food chain are replete with values about what people think is good for themselves, for their community and for society."

Here in Canada, we rely on massive agricultural production, sanitary storage systems and efficient transport networks. But is that wise?

Perhaps 2013 should serve as a cautionary tale. That year, Canadian grain producers experienced near-record yields, but the severe winter storm that put the country on deep-freeze resulted in massive backlogs at the rail terminals. Government action forced the railways to ship a minimum of one million tonnes a week, but there was still grain sitting months later.

Maybe the cross-Canada system we've built is too precarious? With my new source of BC grain, I was now a part of that grain chain, but I wanted a deeper understanding. The following summer, I would begin my ethnographic research as a graduate student at Simon Fraser University. My area of study would be southwestern BC, stretching from Vancouver Island to the Okanagan Valley, including the Sunshine Coast, Vancouver, the Fraser Valley and the Nicola Valley.

↓

"After I found these grain seeds," I tell the kids, "I wanted to learn more about them. About how the seeds are sown, how the stalks grow, how the kernels are harvested and threshed. I wanted to meet and talk with the people who were working and doing these things. So I went back to school—a school called Simon Fraser University. I studied lots about food and farming."

I don't usually tell the kids too much about my research. I save that for my sermons at farmers' markets and conversations with other locavores.

In the local food discourse, a shorter supply chain is usually considered to be better. Buying carrots direct from the farmer, for example, results in the shortest possible food chain: grower to consumer. But in my three years of postgraduate sociology research on southwestern BC grain chains, I began to realize that grain can't be viewed with the same "local food" lens as you would view a carrot. Grain isn't something you can buy from the farm gate and consume directly; it needs infrastructure to move and process it.

This view runs counter to conventional wisdom, where the primary objective of a food supply chain is efficiency. What matters is how fast the food moves from the people who grow it to the people who eat it, and how well each party is compensated along the way. However, in the case of grain chains, while I consider economics an integral part of any analysis, my research suggested that focusing on the almighty dollar isn't the be-all and end-all. If we do that, we will miss the relationships that are formed along the way, the stories that come out of those relationships, and the stories that contribute to and strengthen those relationships.

In addition to being the object of my research, grain became a social tool. I conducted informal interviews, attended lectures and speeches, taught children about grain, took mill tours, drove a combine, cleaned bushels of grain, marvelled at mounds of dough rising in the warmth of bakeries, shared meals with the excited public, dug up lawns to convert them to wheat fields and received sacks or pails of kernels as a means of exchange. In doing this, I experienced what one might call "dynamic relationships"—that is, relationships that can be created or destroyed as a result of people making specific food choices.

The more I learned, the more I wanted to become involved. Not just as an academic with an abstract interest, but as an activist for local grains. So I started by doing something those first BC settlers did 150 years ago: I sowed my own seeds. I ripped open the small brown envelope I had grabbed from a Seedy Saturday event in Vancouver and scattered the seeds in a three-metre by two-metre plot.

To my surprise, it actually grew.

I had seen other small wheat fields in my research, but this small patch was the first I had ever tended from start to finish. I watched it grow, nurtured it, harvested it, threshed it by hand, milled it and made two loaves of bread. I blogged about it and posted photos of my "local-grain initiative."

I was no longer just an ivory tower academic. I was getting down and dirty in the fields, working and singing with friends and community as we sowed, harvested, threshed, milled and baked a "100 percent local grain" whole-wheat pizza crust. It gave me a ground-level perspective on grain chains and how they build and sustain community relationships. And then one day, in late summer 2008, I got a new perspective from the seat of a tractor on Jim's farm in Agassiz, that same farm where I first bought that crop of 100-mile wheat.

I remember the day well. The sun was intense, even as it began its descent behind the mountains. The rattle and whir of the spinning header overpowered the sounds of nature, throwing straw, seeds and chaff up into the air. For a moment I saw the seeds suspended, caught somewhere between plant and harvest. I gazed out into the field ahead and saw the silhouette of a young girl dancing among the short stalks of wheat.

Yelling over the roar of the engine, Jim asked me if I wanted to have a turn driving.

I took my place in the driver's seat and rested my hands on the steering wheel of the red Massey-Harris combine, focusing on keeping a steady hand and cutting a straight edge as we drove from one end of the field to the other. The sound of the cut seed pouring out into the hopper behind me kept me glancing backwards, but Jim told me to keep looking ahead. Keep it straight. Small movements.

Jim had to shout over the noise, but I heard him clearly: "Not too bad, Chris!" Revelling in this pivotal moment, a huge smile spread across my face.

It was on Jim's farm that I learned something important about scale: the mechanization of farming doesn't necessarily mean a loss of connection to the plant, to the soil, to the people.

And it was the merging of those three perspectives—academic, ground-level and tractor-level—that led me on a quest to develop my own kind of agricultural machine: one that was portable, human-powered and performative.

I stop talking, turn my head and look back at the thing behind me under the sheet. I want the kids to see me looking at it, just to remind them that I haven't forgotten. "You've been very patient," I say, "and in a few minutes, we're going to get to the surprise. This is the last part of the story." They squirm with excitement.

"Today, most of our grains are ground in giant mills in Ontario and Quebec, which are even farther away from us than the Prairies are," I tell the kids. "So that means the grain has to travel a long way to get to the mills, and it means the flour has to travel an even longer way to get here. But for centuries before electric mills, before the railways, there were people in every community whose job it was to do the grinding, turning the big heavy stones. Those people had to be strong, but even then, it was a lot of work. So then people figured out they could use their strong animals to turn the wheel. They would get donkeys or horses or other animals to push a bar or pull on a rope, and turn the wheel.

"Yes, you at the back?" I say, pointing to a girl who is waving her hand. "You're right," I respond, "maybe it wasn't very nice to get the animals to do it. But back then, people couldn't think of any other way.

"Eventually, they found ways to harness energy from other sources. Can anyone guess what I'm thinking about? That's right, a windmill; great answer. A windmill is like a big fan that turns when the wind blows, so it uses the earth's free energy to do that heavy work for us. And so when it got windy, people would bring their grain to the miller, and the miller would put the grains inside and grind them up. But windmills only work well in places where the land is flat and wide and windy. They aren't a good idea if you don't have a lot of wind, or if your wind only blows sometimes. So people found a way to turn the grinding stones by using water wheels. That was a bit more reliable than waiting for the wind, because you could use buckets to dump water on them and make the wheel spin whenever you wanted.

"What do your mom and dad's cars run on? That's right, on gas. Some mills started to run on gas, which is a form of energy that you burn to make power. Or they used electricity, which makes your lights and fridge run at your house. Today, most flour is ground in huge mills, in buildings bigger than this gymnasium, with giant rollers crushing and hammers pounding. We use electric energy to do the work of dozens of windmills and waterwheels, hundreds of people and animals.

"But that energy takes money to buy, and using that energy makes some pollution, which is not very good for the earth. So I tried to find a way to grind without that kind of energy—to return to human energy. And besides, I said before that I like freshly ground flour, right? Well, the grain that is milled into flour at those big places gets packed into bags and sent by train across Canada, then it sits in the store until your mom or dad buys it. And then they bring it home, and then maybe you have to wait for a bit until Saturday, when your dad or mom will make you some pancakes. So by the time you eat the first bites, more than two months have passed since it was milled. And maybe your family doesn't get to the bottom of the bag until much later, which means the flour isn't really fresh anymore.

"That's why I bought this hand mill, so I could crank it and grind my flour right before I made my pancakes. But then I thought maybe there is a middle way, a way between using my arm, which gets tired, and using energy like electricity. And then I thought about how my legs were pretty strong—stronger than my arms, anyway. And that's how I got the idea for this..."

Suddenly, I throw back the sheet like a magician and reveal the bike mill.

"Now," I say, as their faces light up, "who wants to go for a ride?"

5

The Bike Mill

When I talk about the bike mill, I use the singular noun. But just to be clear, there were four bike mills built during the Flour Peddler's five years in operation. The first bike mill was built in mid-2008 by a friend named Andrew; that was the bike mill I started grinding on, the one that got me hooked. In mid-2009, I built a second one, then in 2010, a third, and so on. Each one was made to order—I would stumble across a used exercise bike in a thrift shop somewhere, buy it on the spot, heave it into the van and take it home to tinker with—but the underlying form always mirrored Andrew's design: exercise bike, box, belt. And it was a simple design, really. The belt connected directly to the flywheel of the grain mill, which was bolted onto a wooden box. Pedal the contraption and the flywheel spins, and grain comes out.

So when I talk about "the bike mill," I'm not describing any individual contraption so much as explaining the underlying concept behind it. It was like the Platonic forms, I would explain to curious farmers' market shoppers, referencing the Greek philosopher's famous distinction between the specific table you eat on and the idea of a "table" that we all share in our minds—between the abstract and concrete, between the physical world and our metaphysical understanding. It was the symbolism of the bike mill, which could help people re-imagine milling on a human scale, that most appealed to my academic, activist personality. I played the character of a zero-emission community miller, and I used the bike mill as a teaching tool to re-socialize grain—to take it out of the realm of millions of hectares, back to the basics, and bring milling back to the community level.

✷

"Hey, great work, man!" he says to me. "Love the bike mill idea." He stops to talk with me about the bike mill, and then he starts asking about BC grains.

We are on the same page, him and me. That's according to him—he knows it, in fact. We share a vision, he says, about the importance of supporting local farmers and food producers.

You probably know him, or someone like him. He shops at the farmers' market with an almost religious conviction. He's an advocate for all things counterculture. You can tell by how he dresses. In the height of summer, he wears a Balian block-print shirt. In the fall, he's clad in a Bolivian poncho. He sometimes wears a Nepalese beanie, and he wears technical sandals until the first snowfall.

His partner arrives, her arms laden with produce, carrying two cloth bags. He tells her about me and my business, paraphrasing our conversation. She looks at my bike mill and the flour bags on the table.

"That's really interesting," she says. "I grew up on the Prairies where there's more grain than you could ever imagine. But I never really thought about the next stage, you know, the milling side of it. It's strange, really; you sometimes forget there has to be a production phase between the grain and the flour."

She turns to him, motions with her head like she's going off to shop further. She thanks me and leaves.

He talks with me for ten more minutes. We talk about the absurdities of the global food trade, the food miles, the waste. We agree that change has to come from the bottom up, and that ideas like these are an important first start.

He would love to buy a bag and support me, he says, but he's gluten intolerant. He has to be very careful. His exit cue announced, he starts edging away from the table—but he turns back to give me one final thumbs-up before he disappears into the crowd.

A girl wanders away from her mother and comes over to me.

"What's your bike thing?" she asks.

"It's a mill hooked up to a bicycle, and it grinds grains into flour," I say.

Kid: "Can it make pancakes?"

Me: "No, it just grinds up the seeds. See these?" I pour some into the hopper. "We can use the ground-up seeds to make all kinds of yummy things."

Kid: "Can I try?"

Me: "I think you're a bit small to reach the pedals. But do you want to see me grind some grains into flour?"

Kid: "Yeah, that'd be neat."

Me: "Now, watch your hands; don't put them close to the wheel. It would really hurt if you got your finger caught in there. Here we go." Pedalling. "See? That's whole-grain flour. And you can bake with it. Do you like muffins?"

Kid: "Did you make that bike?"

Me: "Yes. I had seen something similar before, but this one is my own design."

Kid: "It looks kind of funny, like bits of different things all stuck together."

Me: "Thanks, that's pretty much what it is. This piece is part of a clothes dryer pipe, like in your laundry room. And this—"

Kid: "Is it heavy and hard to move?"

Me: "Yes, I have to carry it around so I can sell flour at the market. But it's really cool, hey, to show people about milling?"

Mom: "Okay, dear. That's neat, huh? Say thank you to the nice man. Now let's go."

Kid: "But I want to watch it!"

Mom: "No, let's go. Now."

I wave goodbye and chalk up another possible convert.

Sometimes, with parental consent and under close supervision, I would let the taller kids pedal. They usually struggled to get the thing going. The flywheel requires a fair amount of force to initiate the rotation—more than most kids can muster—but once spinning, it requires far less effort to keep it rotating. So sometimes I would spin the pedals by hand for them to get it started.

"Hey," he says, as he approaches my booth. "Did you build this thing yourself?"

He's wearing a yellow racing shirt, black spandex pants and an aerodynamic helmet, even though he's not on a bike at the moment. I saw him coming through the throngs of shoppers. He is high visibility, after all. His special bicycling shoes, the ones that clip into the pedals, click on the pavement. I brace myself.

Bicycle aficionados always wanted to chat. I rarely did, because I knew where the chat would lead.

The flywheel is too small, they would say. Or the drive shaft is too weak. Or it needs a chain rather than a plastic belt. There should be gears on the bike so you can upshift, to make it easier.

Ten minutes later, after pointing out all the flaws they could think of, they would await my response. I would tell them it was just the prototype, and that I was working on a stronger, more efficient model. Maybe it could be fabricated over the winter, and would be done by next season, I suggested.

This was the only fabrication I was going to be doing, a lie I'd invented to explain my lack of technical expertise. But the advice would keep coming: build a strong box with a mill welded to a bike frame, they would say. Ensure a sprocket drives the chain and add a gearshift. It would be easy, they said. I said I thought those were great ideas. Then, having bequeathed their knowledge, they would walk away, the clicking sound fading.

Some, though not all of the bike aficionados saw it for what it was: a ragtag performance prop built by an academic, activist and educator. They saw a good idea—and a botched execution of that idea. They kept telling me what it could be, if only I'd put in the time, effort and money to design, engineer and construct it properly.

One day, I'd say to myself, as they walked away. But I knew I wouldn't. I told myself I didn't have the money to invest, which was true; our bank account was always nearing overdraft. But there was another reason: I had convinced myself I didn't have the knowledge. I hadn't studied physics or technical analysis. I was content to be the Flour Peddler, a farmers' market vendor with a postgraduate sociology degree and an activist streak.

I wasn't an engineer, and I had no interest in becoming one.

Every square metre of Metropolis at Metrotown, the mega-mall in Burnaby, BC, is human-made and maintained. Reflections bounce off shiny store windows, and elevators glide between floors. The colour scheme is explosive: garish purples, lime greens, neon blues. If humanity survives long enough to migrate to outer space, the template for the live-aboard satellites will likely be a mall—an ordered space of temperature regulation and aesthetic uniformity, an advertisement to the civility of the indoor experience, where humans exist independently of the natural world.

Metropolis might as well be on a different planet from the one that spawned the lush, moss-draped rainforest where the Flour Peddler was born. And it's safe to say that normally these two worlds would never meet. But today, March 27, 2009, I'm dragging a large—and very heavy—metal pedal mill along the gleaming tile floors, trying to get to the atrium where I'm supposed to set up and do a grinding demonstration.

An odd juxtaposition, but perhaps that was the intent of the organizers behind the event, which is creatively titled "Agriculture in the City." Billed as a participatory experience to "reconnect" urban shoppers with rural food production activities, it was to feature a full-scale greenhouse, an artificial but anatomically correct cow ready to be "milked," and a stage with cooking demonstrations led by chefs wearing white aprons and wireless microphones.

And the Flour Peddler.

The mill I am dragging today is not one of my creations. It's not made from an exercise bike, but rather is a simple metal frame with pedals and a mill bolted to the front. I've borrowed this mill from Our Community Bikes in Vancouver. It was originally built by an organization called Maya Pedal, a Guatemalan NGO (non-governmental organization) that constructs heavy-duty *bici-machinas* (bicycle machines) including corn mills, fruit blenders, even washing machines.

I had elected not to bring my bike mill from home. The design made it finicky, and I wasn't confident it would perform as required, especially in front of a crowd. I was scheduled to be grinding grain for the pancake demo later this afternoon, and I knew I would need something heavy-duty.

I'm excited about the demonstration, but it's a long way to the atrium, I think, as I struggle to drag the mill.

The mall understands humanity's desire to consume, and it zones accordingly. Planners know the importance of keeping retail space separate from food production. The food court—a sparkling world where mass-produced plastic trays transport mass-produced food-like substances from grill to table to waste receptacle—is segregated from the other shops.

At 10:00 a.m. sharp, I hop on the bike mill to do a two-minute demonstration in an attempt to draw a crowd. I'm not sure if the shoppers will be receptive to my academic or activist views, but at least they can't help noticing me. With the wheels spinning, gears turning, chains rattling and steel plates grinding together, I'm the loudest display by far.

An hour later, I've made a lot of noise and pedalled out four kilograms of flour. But not one shopper has come over to talk or even to ask questions. Some watch me for a few moments from a distance, some walk in a wider arc to avoid me, while others snap cellphone photos, then continue quickly on.

The bike mill is my trump card, but I suppose it can't compete with a robotic cow.

"That's really loud, you know," one lady shouts over the noise of the grinding plates. "Far too loud!"

I try to tell her I'm an integral part of the event, but she puts her fingers in her ears and walks away.

"Chris!" William calls out to me as he approaches through the food court, with a smile that seems as wide as the atrium. "Is this the pedal mill you were telling me about?"

William is wearing a purple shirt, black pants and a huge ring of keys on his belt loop. He used to tell Josh and me that he had a key to every door in Metropolis. William had arrived as a refugee in 1994 and worked his way from a job clearing trays in the Metropolis food court to one in the maintenance department. He now walked along to a key-jingling soundtrack like a landlord.

I hadn't been able to contact William in advance to tell him I was going to be at Metropolis this weekend. But I had hoped he would hear about me—or quite literally hear the bike mill—and stop by for a visit.

"Chris," he says, after watching me grind flour for a few minutes, "this pedal mill is a great idea, especially for places with no electricity. You know, I think this could work in my home village."

I smile. "That sounds like fun."

"I've got to get back to work," William says, clasping my hand as he turns to go. "But maybe someday you will bring this bike-mill machine to my home village!"

It's an enticing idea. But I put it in the back of my mind, alongside other ideas like trekking in Tajikistan or enrolling in a Romanian circus school to indulge my long-standing interest in juggling, both implausible scenarios at this point in my life.

While I was fascinated by William's stories of Africa, back then I was a pretty committed Latin American traveller. I liked a breezy veranda and an aquamarine sea, a hammock and a glass of rum, the odd cigar and the opportunity to use the Spanish I had worked hard to learn. So whenever William talked about life in his village—and how he hoped to one day return to his country, which he was sure would someday be the independent country of South Sudan—I would imagine a barren desert with skinny cows, mud huts and not a coffee or a swimming hole to be found.

Over the following four years, I built four different bike mills. Some were clearly better than others; it all depended on how sturdy the exercise bike was, how low it was to the ground, how stable it was when I stood up and pedalled. My kids, Solomon and Gretchen, gave each one of the bike mills nicknames, making sure they were welcomed as new additions to the family.

But by September 2012, the bike mill had spun its last market. I told the kids it had been put out to pasture, but taken behind the barn and put out of its misery was probably more accurate. At this point, Josh and I had stopped doing the farmers' markets and were concentrating on our monthly home delivery. We no longer needed the component pieces to assemble the bike mill, and so the rusting exercise bike sat under my porch. Occasionally, Gretchen would drag it out and climb up on it, forgetting that the seat cushion was saturated with rainwater, and then squeal as she hopped off, her pants soaked through.

By 2013, William had done just as he said he would and returned to the newly formed country of South Sudan. We called him in March and told him we wanted to come to South Sudan. That's great, he replied, the line crackling. And we told him we wanted to build a bike mill for his village, like the one we had for the grinding business. He said he remembered it very well, like it was yesterday, and confirmed that this was great news indeed. We said we wanted to come in December. The perfect time to visit, he remarked, not too hot yet. All we needed now, we told him, was to raise money to hire workers in South Sudan to build it.

We launched the Flour Peddler International crowdfunding campaign on the morning of June 3, 2013, with a goal of thirty-five hundred dollars—the bare minimum we figured we'd need to cover on-the-ground expenses in South Sudan. We were planning to travel with the Country Living Grain Mill and a few sprockets, and buy everything else on site. We would buy the materials locally, pay local people to build the bike mill, and then pay to transport it to William's village. We didn't know exactly how this would happen, of course, but we figured it wouldn't be cheap.

Over the next three weeks, we raised $350, mostly from a sale we held in the basement of the First Lutheran Church in Vancouver. But we had an ace up our sleeve: publicity. Randy Shore, the food columnist from the *Vancouver Sun*, had written a story on the Flour Peddler back in 2010. I had talked to Randy on the bus into Vancouver a few months before we launched our crowdfunding campaign, and I told him about our South Sudan bike-mill project. He interviewed me in late May for a follow-up story. He didn't know when it would run, he told me, but he figured early June.

Early June came and went, and the crowdfunding account stayed at $350, no matter how much we pushed it on social media. But then, on the morning of June 27, 2013, there we were in the Technology section of the Saturday paper: a full-page story about the Hergesheimer brothers and their upcoming trip to South Sudan, titled "BC inventor tackles poverty in South Sudan with bike-powered grain mill."

That morning, we had promised to take our cousin Mike, who was visiting from Arizona, to a secret coastal gem—an organic pitch-and-putt golf course carved out of the blackberry bushes on private land in Wilson Creek. On the drive there, Josh read the story to me, over and over again, from the back seat.

I had just hit a great pitching wedge shot when my phone buzzed: a $250 donation had just appeared on our crowdfunding page. I turned to Josh. "It's on now, bro," I said, smiling, and showed him the donations page. We high-fived, and ended the day with $1,700. "Well," Josh said, with a mixture of excitement and trepidation, "now we're really going to have to figure out how to build this."

Josh was right. With this money came responsibility. Before, it was "our money." We were using the profits from the sale of our grains to buy the airline tickets. But this was different; it was money given for a purpose, donated by people who were backing our efforts to build this bike mill. Now that we had supporters, we couldn't let them down. I went to sleep that night, full of excitement and worry.

The next morning, there was an email message in the Flour Peddler inbox from a man named Christopher Douglas, the founder and managing director of Lone Star Africa Works, a Texas-based non-profit that operates in South Sudan. The email asked us to get in touch, so Josh dialed the number.

"That article in the Vancouver paper about your bike mill showed up on my newsfeed," he told Josh, "and I just had to talk to you." Josh thanked him for making the connection. "So why did you guys choose South Sudan?" Douglas asked. Josh told him about William. "I like your idea a lot," Douglas replied, "but South Sudan is a really tough country in which to do something like this. I don't even know where you'd get scrap metal that wouldn't set you back a fortune. A lot of welders don't have gas, and who knows whether the drill presses have bits. In fact, no one has much of anything—for cheap, that is. If you want to spend a ton of money, well then, South Sudan is your place."

Josh winced, thanked him and said we'd be in touch. Douglas said he'd ask around the next time he passed through Juba, which would be later that summer.

One month later, Lone Star Africa Works sent us a link to a photo stream. I clicked on it, and up popped a dozen photos of a metal shop in Juba! With tools!

In the accompanying email, Douglas said he had found a place we might be interested in. It was a technical school—not a college, but a high school where young people from across the country learned trade skills. There were classes in brickmaking, woodwork, mechanics and metalwork. He had seen the welding shop, and while it wasn't clear to him if they had propane for the torches or gas for the generator, he was pretty sure that this was a place where we could build a bike mill.

We stopped reading the email and started thinking out loud. This was the place, we told ourselves excitedly. As long as we could raise enough money, we could hire professionals to construct it. It would be a way to support local talent, we reasoned, and it would inject a few hundred dollars into the local economy. Besides, they could tailor the design and engineering specs to the local conditions; they would know what parts were available and how to work with whatever they had. Only they could build a bike mill strong enough to stand up to the rigours of life in rural South Sudan.

It would be amazing, we agreed. In fact, it would be the best bike mill ever.

The email concluded with a link to Plan International, an NGO whose name Douglas had seen on a sign at the technical college. Josh searched the web and sent several emails to their South Sudan office, but never received confirmation that they knew we were coming.

As our departure date drew closer with no response from the technical school, I had the nagging fear that we would arrive to an empty school or arrive to find out they wouldn't be able to help us. Josh tried to assuage my concern by adding "Appointment @ Technical School" to our travel itinerary, scheduling it for the second day and telling me not to worry. "Somehow it will work out," he said, trying to emulate the tone of an Enlightened One. "In Africa, things rarely work the way you plan, but something always works out in the end."

By early November, however, we were both getting anxious. It was only a month until departure, and we had no confirmation from the Juba Technical School that they knew we were coming, let alone that they were willing to help us. Maybe our mid-December arrival date meant the school would be closed for Christmas?

We knew we couldn't just show up and hope to make it work. The people who supported our crowdfunding campaign were relying on us to give it our best shot. We had to make the transition from abstract theory (academic community miller, food security activist, and grain educator) to reality (rural life in a place far from mills or repair shops). We had to become what we had never wanted to be: engineers.

Josh and I set up the exercise bicycle in the yard. It looked sad and lonely. Then I hauled over the wooden box, the mill still bolted on top. I positioned the box just behind the exercise bike, in its usual spot. We stepped back and stared at it.

"It's an exercise bike, positioned behind a freestanding box," Josh said, as if to no one in particular. "It's so simple."

"Maybe," I counter. "But it's the stability that's important."

"The stability comes from the exercise bike," he replied. "It's an integral part of the design." We thought a bit more.

"Somehow, I don't think we'll be able to find any used exercise bikes in South Sudan," I said.

"That's true. But we could probably buy a used bicycle in Kampala."

I thought about this. "We could remove the wheels, bend the frame and use the pedal mechanism of the bicycle," I said, mentally going through the process.

"Or maybe," Josh said, now speeding along, "we could attach the mill behind the seat, like to the luggage rack at the back? Then it would be right above the back sprocket, and would pull straight down. Keep the pedals and chain as is, just add a second chain between the mill and the sprocket on the back wheel."

"A horizontal chain to pedal and turn the wheel—"

"—and a vertical chain to drive the grinder," he finished the sentence.

We looked at each other. It was truly a brotherly moment.

"That could actually work," he said.

I felt the excitement surge through my body. "And maybe, if it was built well enough and welded properly, people could actually ride it, like to a market."

"That would be amazing," he said.

It was quiet for a while. Then I broke the silence. "How would we ever do it?"

"We need some technical advice," Josh answered.

The next morning, Josh contacted the Applied Science Technologists and Technicians of BC and asked them to run this ad in their email newsletter:

Calling all technicians, technologists, technophiles and pedal-power enthusiasts!

You may recall a story in the Vancouver Sun about two BC brothers travelling to South Sudan to build a bicycle mill :http://www.vancouversun.com/business/inventor+tackles+poverty+South+Sudan+with+bike+powered+grain+-mill/8588319/story.html

Let's cut to the chase: we want you! We are asking for any technophile out there who can contribute their expertise, insights and—just maybe!—a little elbow grease to help us build a prototype before we depart for South Sudan on December 7.

For five years, we've been using our bicycle grinder at farmers' markets around the Lower Mainland. In that time we've built several versions of our pedal-powered grinder, but each time we've relied on a simple design: an exercise bicycle with a belt that attaches to a grain mill sitting on a large wooden box. Pedal the exercise bike, the mill turns, and out comes freshly ground grain. You can see a video of our bicycle-mill "creation" here: http://vimeo.com/6867960

However, this design does not "internationalize" well, as there are no old (or new) exercise bikes where we are going. There are, however, plenty of old bicycles in East

Africa, so our plan is to travel carrying only the mill and some bicycle parts (sprockets, chains, small wrenches, etc.), buy an old bicycle frame either in Uganda or South Sudan, and work with locals to build the bike mill on site.

The problem? We can't figure out how to use the rear-wheel-drive system found on bicycles rather than the front-wheel drive found on exercise bikes. One option would be to use a sprocket from an 18-speed bicycle: run a chain horizontally from the pedals to the sprocket, and another vertically from the sprocket to the flywheel of the mill. (We would have to attach a sprocket to the flywheel for this to work, and somehow attach the mill to the seat post.)

Anyone with something to contribute is welcome to get in touch. What would be most helpful is if someone could spare a few hours to work through the design and construction process with us, as well as brainstorm through the challenges and obstacles we are likely to come up against in South Sudan.

Thanks for your help!

A few hours later, a response landed in the Flour Peddler inbox.

"Just keep it simple," David Sawley says when I meet him at his waterfront office in Gibsons a week later. A member of the Applied Science Technologists and Technicians of BC, David isn't keen on our double sprocket idea. "Too complicated," he says. "Better to just run one chain from the pedal mechanism straight to the flywheel." He draws a simple right-angle triangle set-up with the chain as the hypotenuse. "You've got to think about the force exerted, and the direction of pull."

I stare at the sketch on the paper. I pretty much understand the physics of what he's suggesting, but I have no idea how we'd actually engineer this in real life. I imagine Josh and me somewhere in a sun-baked desert with greasy hands and the wrong-sized wrench, throats parched and carrion birds circling overhead—the two of us struggling to bolt something onto something else, and failing miserably.

"And whatever you do, don't make it too complex or flashy," he concludes. I thank him and leave the office. Don't worry, David— little chance of that.

The sunshine outside momentarily blinds me. When I entered the office, it was drizzling, but now there's a break in the clouds, just enough for a ray of sun to sneak through. I stop a moment, warming my body from the chill in the air. I call Josh, tell him that I've received some good advice from David and try to sound upbeat. "I know we can do this," I say, though I'm not much more sure than I was an hour ago.

"That's great, bro," Josh replies. "I'm stuck in the planning and logistics. Hopefully you can take on the bike mill side of things. Getting info on the entry visa and the import requirements is more complicated than I thought."

I'm not pleased with how he just did that—palmed the technical side of things off on me, as if I know anything about how this is going to work. "Okay, cool," I lie. I hang up the phone and take a deep breath of the salty sea air. Seagulls swoop, circling around Winegarden Waterfront Park and Gibsons Harbour.

I really hope this works.

6

The Juba Technical School

"So, I'll just leave you guys here, then," William says as he puts down the box. "Someone will come." He turns and walks back down the dirt road that leads out the gate of the Juba Technical Secondary School. I look around, but I don't see any students, any teachers, anyone really, except for some random kids who've come here to check us out. It's pretty quiet here.

I don't want William to leave. When we are with him, things are easy: we are introduced, our situation explained. People smile and doors open. Like this door, for example—the door of the school's office. It's locked, and no one is here. But even if someone was here, I'm not sure I could actually explain myself. If William stayed with us, at least we would have a hope.

What if the headmaster doesn't arrive? Or what if he does show up but he can't accommodate us? We did just arrive in this country, hoping to get some help building something we ourselves don't adequately understand.

I turn to Josh. "We'd better hope this pans out."

"I know," he answers.

Fifteen minutes later, Headmaster John Manas arrives, a jovial man with greying hair. "I remember hearing about your visit through one of the NGO workers who said they received an email from you," he says as he shakes my hand. I tell him I'm very happy to meet him, which is the truth.

"But I seem to recall it was going to be sometime next year," he continues. Oh no, this can't be happening. Clearly, the lines of communication had been crossed somewhere along those fibre optic cables.

"Well," I offer cautiously, "we are here now, and we only have two days before we have to travel to Aweil. If there is someone here who can give us access to a drill press and a welding machine, and contribute their technical knowledge, we would be more than pleased to provide the school and staff with some compensation."

I've played my trump card already, but his reaction isn't as exuberant as I'd hoped.

He mumbles and shuffles some papers on his desk. "Let me think," he says, as he slides opens one drawer, then another. I look over at Josh, who signals to me that we should wait outside. Now that we have a foot in the door, I don't want to leave, but I sense the "softly softly" approach might yield better results.

We leave the office, carry the disassembled bicycle to a flat surface and cut open the woven bag. I grab some tools and start tinkering around with the bolts, trying to keep busy so I don't focus on the fact that this is pretty much our only chance. Without this shop and its expertise, there's no way we can pull this off.

A few tall boys in long dark-blue coveralls with black stains gather around, hands behind their backs. I can feel them watching me, this white guy who arrived with a bicycle in a bag, and I can't even seem to get the pieces out of the bag properly. I start feeling anxious. I wonder, would it be better to appear as though we know what we are doing, or to be upfront about our woeful lack of expertise and hope they take pity on us and help?

The headmaster appears at the door as I struggle to push the back wheel past the brake pad. He chuckles. "So you have some business in Canada with a pedal mill, that is correct?"

I nod, my lips pursed, frustration building below the surface as I fiddle with the knobs on the derailleur and tug on the chain. "Yes, that's right," I say, and then wince as I pinch my finger. "But we've never constructed one with a bicycle before." I fumble with a wrench, and it clatters onto the cement.

"I have called the manager of the welding shop," the headmaster says. "He will come, and you can converse with him about the possibilities."

I stop what I'm doing, stand up and take a deep breath. I look around for Josh and see that he's off taking photos of the schoolyard. "Sit down," the headmaster says, offering a chair. "You are obviously tired from a long journey." I fall into the chair and take a swig of water.

Thirty-five minutes later, a red motorcycle rolls into the yard. The driver takes off his helmet and shakes my hand, smiling when he hears my name. "This is a fortunate coincidence," he says, "for my name is also Christopher." He walks towards the metal shop, fishes a key ring from his pocket, clicks the padlock and slides the large metal doors open.

The workshop is silent. Chunks of scrap metal lean against the walls, sections of pipe are stacked in corners. I start to head inside, but the tall boys in the coveralls hold me back. "Wait, please," one says. I step back, and a young boy with a broom heads inside and starts sweeping. The other boys fan out and start opening the windows and doors. "Sit under the tree," another offers, gesturing to a low tree with wide branches near the back of the yard. There are brightly painted wooden slats forming benches under the boughs. Josh, now back from his photo shoot at the schoolyard, heads towards it, but I'm too excited to leave the doorway.

I knew it would all work out!

Ten minutes later, the young boy with the broom departs. "Thanks!" I shout to him, but he doesn't turn around. Josh and I break open the cardboard box and start unpacking the sprockets, derailleurs, various pedal bars and chains we'd picked up at Our Community Bikes in Vancouver. I spread out the cheap wrenches and socket sets from the New Westminster Army and Navy, as if they would be needed. The boys stop what they are doing and watch.

I grab a sprocket set and hold it up next to the flywheel of the grain mill to show Christopher the basic idea. He pauses, says something in Juba Arabic, and the boys head over to the generator. One rips on the starting cord while another bends over a power bar and starts inserting chunky black plugs. The generator chugs to life, belching black, sooty smoke. The boys pull their shirts up over their mouths and noses and continue while Josh and I head for the door.

After the black haze dissipates, we re-enter and see Christopher with one knee down on the floor and the grain mill on its side. A tap, then a *click-click-crackle-sizzle*, and sparks fly as the welding begins. After a few minutes, someone heads off and returns carrying a welding mask. Christopher holds the mask about six inches from his face with one hand, the welding torch in the other. Josh tries to get an up-close photo, but shuffles back when a spark bounces onto his arm. He settles for arm's-length and snaps away.

I step back for a second, watch the firework sparkle created by the welding torch. The generator's noise is nearly deafening, its exhaust now flowing out the door and window behind it. I look at the jerry cans beside it, half-filled with gas—gas that will need to be poured into this beast to power the shop.

It's a strange way to build a zero-emissions bike mill, I admit. But then life in Juba, it seems, is full of contradictions.

Juba's rapid growth and new-found wealth have created this city of paradoxes along the White Nile. The paved roads are lined with bustling shops and multi-storey buildings, but the back streets are dirt tracks with deep potholes that fill like swimming pools after the rain. Many residents subsist on two US dollars a day, while expats rent concrete-box apartments for two hundred a night. After the Comprehensive Peace Agreement that ended the Second Sudanese Civil War was signed, nearly ten years previously, there was an influx of United Nations staff and expatriate workers, all of whom needed accommodation in Juba. Entrepreneurs cashed in, and as contractors began building apartments and hotels, they were snapped up for absurd sums of money. In 2011, after the country officially separated from Sudan, Juba became the capital of newly independent South Sudan, attracting an army of oil workers, overseas investors and aid workers—a trend that shows no signs of slowing despite political instability, corruption and violence.

An expatriate website recommended budgeting at least $150 US per night for a Juba hotel that would meet international standards. For even more money, you can sleep in converted shipping containers stacked on top of each other. If you're on an expense account, the sky's the limit. On the low end of the scale, the cheapest hotel Josh had heard about was seventy-five dollars, and it was rumoured to have dank rooms, sporadic electricity and dodgy plumbing. WiFi was definitely not included.

Thankfully, William had sensed our budgetary constraints and brought us to the American Hotel. Or the Americana Hotel, depending on whether you go by the sign in front of the hotel—a strange rendition of Old Glory fluttering behind an Eiffel Tower— or the sign over the restaurant door. A flock of goats nibbled at smouldering garbage outside the gate, but we stepped into an Eritrean paradise.

The owner told us to call him Sammy, and his wife—a glamorous woman with hair curls that bounced as she moved—was only too happy to sell us cold beer. William suggested we see the rooms upon arrival, but we suggested a round of drinks instead. Josh and William cracked Tuskers, but I asked for a Bell, the Ugandan beer I'd developed a taste for in the forty hours since our plane had landed.

The rooms were immaculately clean, with decorative white and blue window trim. The toilet flushed and water came out of the showerhead. The bed was draped with a mosquito net, and the fan on the wall was locked in the ideal position to keep guests cool. Outside, posters of Eritrean pop stars plastered the small courtyard, where several other guests sat eating *injera* (flatbread) with their fingers and sipping tiny coffees to a soundtrack of Tigrigna love songs.

When I heard the price, I almost laughed: forty US dollars a night, but no discounts for extended stays. The best part? Less than a five-minute walk from the Juba Technical Secondary School.

As Christopher finishes welding the sprocket onto the flywheel of the mill, we gather around to discuss the next steps. Josh holds the seat of the mountain bike so it stays upright, and I try to explain our plan: somehow attach the mill onto the back luggage rack so a chain can drive it from the wheel.

"Too complicated," Christopher says, echoing the words David said to me back in his Gibsons office three weeks earlier. "That would take some serious engineering. But I have another idea."

Christopher says something, and the boys set to work, using the metal saw to cut various lengths of hollow metal bars. Other boys dig through the pile of old metal desks. After two hours, they have built a tall rectangular frame that encompasses the back wheel, a bit wider at the bottom than the top for stability. "The frame should hold the mill above the bike's back wheel," Christopher explains. "Then all we have to do is figure out how to run a chain to connect the flywheel to the sprocket."

But try as we might, we can't make it work. The frame has only been spot welded, since we're still brainstorming the design at this point, and it wobbles when we hold the mill above it. One of the spot welds breaks off, and the metal bars clank to the cement floor.

Christopher doesn't say it, but I get the feeling his idea won't work either. He senses that I'm losing confidence, so he takes me by the shoulder and says, "Don't worry. Here in Africa, we are used to being creative with whatever we have."

I smile. "But now," he says, "it's lunchtime. We will continue after our break."

While the students break for lunch, Josh and I decide to wander. At first we stick to the main dirt roads around the school, but soon we are drawn into the narrow sandy tracks that lead into the dense network of huts across the road. Though we're only a few hundred metres from a paved road, this section of shacks and huts feels like a village on the outskirts of nowhere. Pots of boiling millet burble on charcoal stoves, which are set on packed-dirt entrance-ways, while kids dart in and out of doors, some squealing with delight at the sight of us, others hiding their faces in the laps of mothers and grandmothers. "*Khawaji! Khawaji!*" they yell—the Arabic term used to label white foreigners in South Sudan. Occasionally, I wink at a child, sending the little boy or girl giggling and running.

Out of the corner of my eye, I see a white pickup skid to a stop on the dirt road nearby. Men in suits jump out, slam the doors and head in our direction.

"Good day, gentlemen," I say, trying to appear calm.

"What are you doing here, in this place?" snaps one man.

"Just walking around, seeing the life in Juba," Josh quickly responds, with an air of calm that escapes me. The other men watch me, but sometimes glance at Josh's camera. Josh notices and rests his arm over it.

I panic, imagining the arrest: Josh and I bundled into the back of an unmarked pickup, taken to a cement interrogation room in a compound somewhere. No one knows where we are. The boys at the welding shop would never come looking for us. William would eventually, but where would he even start?

The tallest and baldest man scowls. "You should not be moving around here in such an insecure fashion."

I give him a look like I'm surprised. "Is it not safe here?" I say, though I realize that may not have been a good choice of words.

He stares at me for a few seconds, then blurts out, "Who can say?" Neither Josh nor I are sure if this is a question or a statement, so we say nothing.

"You must return directly to your place of residence," he says, after considering the matter.

"We will," I quickly reply, "and thank you very much, gentlemen."

It's 5:00 p.m. and Josh and I crack our second beer—him, Tusker and me, Bell—in the tiny courtyard of the American Hotel.

I fish a sanitary wipe out of the package that Josh has brought, and start cleaning my face and hands with it. It feels great to be cleansed of the grease and grime of the metal shop. I'll wait until tonight to take a shower, then head straight to bed. Josh looks over at me, confused. "Chris, those are the electronic wipes for my computer screen," he says, stifling a laugh.

I pause and then carry on, though I stay away from my face. "They are clearly double-duty wipes."

I'm trying to remain upbeat. After a full day at the Technical School, we've determined that the rear-wheel-drive bike-mill idea is too complicated. Christopher and his assistants have tried to build a platform behind the rear wheel to bolt the mill onto, but we can't figure out the next step: connecting the chain from the rear wheel to the flywheel of the mill. We've used up one of the two days we had allotted for construction of the mill, so if we don't get it completed tomorrow, then what?

William sees us looking disheartened. "Cheer up, guys," he says. "It will be fine." William is always so optimistic! I smile a tired smile and nod. "Besides," he says, "tonight we are going to Tong Ping, to meet my friends for a barbeque."

He's right. An hour later, we're sitting in an outdoor bar in Tong Ping, an upscale district of Juba, waiting for the goat to arrive, and we're both feeling great.

It could be the beer, of course. Bottles line the table, all available brands represented—Tusker, Heineken and, of course, Bell for me—while flames lick the hunks of meat grilling on the oil-drum barbeque. The generator is *ta-ta-ta-tatting* in the corner, powering the large-screen television, which broadcasts the Kenyan celebrations marking fifty years since independence. The sound is turned up for the speeches, and as each politician and statesman takes his turn at the microphone, William and his friends call out like announcers at a hockey game.

"Yes! Such quality oration from these chaps!" William's friend Morris claps heartily, then leans over to me. "This is what we fought for," he tells me. "These Kenyan chaps have had fifty years to get their act together. And now, Kenyans are doing it for themselves. Imagine our country, South Sudan, fifty years from now." His voice fills with optimism. "With all the skills we have, and with the world's help, how can we not succeed?"

"To South Sudan at fifty?" I suggest, raising my bottle.

Morris agrees. "To South Sudan at fifty!" We clink bottles. I get up, ask William if I can borrow his phone. According to my time-zone calculations, it's morning in Roberts Creek, so I want to try calling Amanda-Rae and the kids. The line beeps as the connection is made; her voice crackles. "Chris?" she says. "Where are you? It sounds like the inside of an engine."

I walk to the corner of the yard, trying to put some distance between me and the generator. Amanda-Rae and I exchange a few sentences, but I'm struggling to hear her voice over the noise. We haven't really connected since I left six days ago, and that's a long time for us. I'm longing to hear her voice, her laugh. I feel so far away—far away from her, my kids, my home, my friends, the forests of Roberts Creek. A first time in Africa is something that impacts even a seasoned traveller in its own particular way, and I have so much to tell her.

I turn around when a server passes carrying a gigantic platter. On top is a pyramid of charred meat and bones. Morris shouts to me, "Tell your woman you must return her call, after you have eaten African goat on African fire!"

Never missing an opportunity for celebration, Josh raises his bottle. "To African goat on African fire!" The group cheers. I tell Amanda-Rae I will call her back when I find somewhere quieter. William's familiar laughter roars across the yard and I feel a moment of ease. I head back to the table and sit down. It's been a few years since I started eating meat again, which definitely makes travel moments like this more enjoyable. I sit down, grabbing the bowed end of a bone and gnawing the succulent flesh. Ten minutes later, the pile has nearly vanished, and we're all sitting back, licking our fingers and passing around toothpicks.

Morris calls for another round of beers. After all that meat, I really don't feel like drinking, but on cue, a serving tray arrives bearing beer bottles, followed by a chorus of bottle caps clattering through the gaps in the tables and landing in the dirt. With no menus or price lists anywhere, only locals know what any of this costs, and I'm starting to worry. I lean over to William. "Will you please keep track of what we owe? Josh and I want to contribute our fair share."

William laughs. "When you drink with Morris, more often than not, Morris will pay."

I wince. I was worried he might say this. "William," I reply, lowering my voice, "we came here with the expectation that we would buy our own food and drinks. Josh and I have money budgeted—not a lot, but enough—and we don't want to be seen to take without giving."

William smiles. "Chris, I know you have this way of thinking, but that is not how it works here. You are a visitor to South Sudan, so everyone wants to show you hospitality. It is part of our culture; even if you visit the poorest people in the most remote village, they will share what little they have with a guest. And besides," he adds, "Morris has a good job at the KCB bank. The people who do finance jobs in Juba, they are paid well."

It's nearing midnight, and most of the bar's patrons have dispersed. Morris says, to no one in particular, "Those responsible chaps have headed out at a sensible hour. It's the price one pays for opting into the daily grind." I'm feeling drunk and woozy from the jet lag. Morris leans over and clasps my hand. "A sincere thank you for the time you and your brother have shared with us tonight. It has been quite stimulating to speak with you on varying topics as the evening has permitted," he says. "Before you depart, one more for the road?"

I laugh, shaking my head, but Morris is already flipping the top off another Bell. I glance imploringly at William, and he intervenes. "We gladly accept your offer," William says as he rises from his chair, "but these gentleman must take their final beverage to go, quite literally, for the road." Josh and I get up, shake everyone's hands, and then make our way towards William's truck, carrying our bottles.

As William guides the pickup truck through the dark roads to the American Hotel, I gush about Morris's infectious optimism and, above all, his generosity. William smiles. "It's just like how your mom and dad host those big dinners for Easter and Christmas," he tells me. "For as long as I can remember, your parents have invited everyone who does not have their own family to eat with them, to tell stories with them, to share time with each other." It sounds like he's dining out on the memory. "Each year, I would arrive at the door, and your mom would serve more and more—there was never an end to the food. There would be ham and then chicken and also potatoes and fresh green beans..." I can tell William is savouring the flavours in his mind, and I start doing it too.

I imagine Mom and Dad at home, the gas fireplace roaring in the winter. I think of those big family dinners and how William was there at each and every one, without fail.

"And even what I could not eat, she would send home with me," William continues. "Your mom would pile the food into containers that I would take for my next dinner, my dinner after that, and always enough for my roommates. For days after being at your parents' house, I would open my fridge, and containers with tinfoil would greet me! She is so generous, your mom."

I reflect on it: something so simple, yet so integral, and so often taken for granted. It's the connection between food and family—sharing, socializing, building relationships—that people like Morris don't have, or can't have, living in Juba. Morris's wife and kids live in Nairobi, Kenya, five hundred kilometres away, where there are affordable apartments and good schools for the kids. Thanks to Morris's work in Juba, he can support them, but this also means he can only visit them once every few months. So sharing food and drinks with friends, especially old friends like William, is about the closest he can get to a family dinner.

I fall asleep that night thinking about Mom and her heavenly Easter dinners.

V

The next morning, I'm on the move.

The wind whips my hair as Christopher cracks open the throttle. I'm sitting on the back seat of his motorcycle, leaning over his right shoulder as we thread through Juba's bustling streets. After several twists and turns, we leave the pavement and bounce down a sandy track that leads to the Konyo Konyo market, a labyrinth of hand-built shops made of plywood and corrugated metal, and packed with vendors, shoppers and pickpockets. Christopher suggests I move my backpack to my chest and stay close.

We arrive at a shop selling bike parts, where a group of men dissecting motorcycles stare at me. Speaking Juba Arabic, Christopher asks about pedals, bearings, grease. I hand over 140 South Sudanese pounds, and one of the guys hands me a plastic bag full of parts. We stop again at a liquor store that also sells bike seats. We buy one seat and a set of handlebars for forty pounds.

"Now," Christopher says, "we go and build your pedal machine."

We had originally intended to attach the mill to the bicycle, using the pedals to drive the sprocket welded to the flywheel. But after a day spent welding, sawing and sweating, Christopher and I elected to change the design. What we really needed was to weld the pedal mechanism to a strong rectangular metal frame. A simple, solid design.

Six hours later, it is done: a large metal cube with a pedal mechanism, a seat, handlebars and a platform where the Country Living Grain Mill will be bolted on. Once the guys at the Juba Technical Secondary School figured out the design, it came together like clockwork, and the finished product is nothing short of amazing.

Nothing fancy—just like David had advised us three weeks ago in Gibsons.

That evening, we celebrate our success at an Ethiopian restaurant along the banks of the Nile. As we wait for the *injera* flatbread and beef *tibs*, I see a man on the restaurant dock with a narrow dugout canoe. I ask William if we can hire him to take us for a ride, but he waves me off.

"The river is too fast," he says. "If you tip, you will float all the way down through Uganda into Lake Victoria, near where your plane landed." He adds, laughing, "All your struggles on Baby Coach would have been for nothing."

"Speaking of Baby Coach," I start in.

Earlier that day, Josh and I had decided we needed to talk to William about the next step: how to get from Juba to Panlang. William's home village wasn't exactly close to Juba. In fact, it was as far north as you could go in South Sudan before you run up against Darfur on the Sudanese border, nearly seven hundred kilometres away, according to Josh's map. The road from Juba started out on the map as a thick black line, then got thinner and thinner, then dotted, before the lines just disappeared. We would need to travel to Rumbek, then Wau, then Aweil, then to Marial Bai, made famous by the novel *What Is the What: The Autobiography of Valentino Achak Deng*, by Dave Eggers. A few more kilometres south was the village of Panlang.

"My brother, that road is bad!" William roars with laughter when we tell him we want to go overland. "You soft Canadian boys, you will not survive. It will take several days driving in a *matatu* transport van to get to Aweil." He reaches in his pocket and pulls out his phone. "I have made other arrangements."

Given the tight time frame, Josh and I concede we need to fly one direction between Juba and Aweil. We tell William we will purchase the return ticket from Aweil to Juba for December 19. We hand him three crisp US one-hundred-dollar bills to pay for the tickets: two one-way tickets, we insist. William waves us off, saying we wouldn't need any tickets because of his "other arrangements." He won't tell us what these other arrangements are, so we keep trying to convince him about the importance of a backup plan. Eventually, William calls Morris and asks him to book us two tickets from Aweil to Juba on December 19—six days from now.

The return journey sorted, we reiterate to William that we want to go overland from Juba to Panlang. What a trip it would be, we told him excitedly, from the subtropical shores of Lake Victoria to the far reaches of northern South Sudan!

"You guys," he says. "It's extremely uncomfortable and crowded, and it will take at least sixty hours." We didn't really expect that William would understand. Why would we want to spend three days and nights in a cramped van with a dozen other people and their luggage, after all? William couldn't appreciate the depth of our commitment to going overland, our desire to struggle all the way to our final destination. He couldn't understand that we were willing to suffer for a few more days, as long as they were the last days we would ever suffer on behalf of the Flour Peddler. For the past year, I've imagined how good it will feel to set up the bike mill under a tree in William's village—and then to say goodbye, and watch it fade in the rear-view mirror as we drive away. From there on out, we would tell the story of the Flour Peddler in the past tense. No longer would riding a bike mill define me. It would be what I did, not what I do.

And what relief that change of tense would be! No more half-dozing at the Langdale ferry terminal in line for the 6:20 a.m. Saturday sailing. No more setting up the rusty tent, praying it would survive to erect another day. No more sprinting to a supermarket to break a twenty-dollar bill and collect coins for the float. No more digging through crumpled grain bags in the trunk, searching for an elusive red-spring label. All the stress that comes with the farmers' market life would evaporate. And all the disappointment that comes from knowing your business is destined for failure—and all the psychological torment that comes from continuing to operate that failing business—would disappear.

That feeling would be worth the effort it would take to go overland, we agreed. Besides, Josh and I reasoned, we had somehow survived Baby Coach—the way the underdog kids' sports team somehow emerges victorious—and we were confident in our ability to endure whatever the journey threw at us. We were like athletes who, in the heat of competition, surpass their own expectations, surprising themselves. If we made it this far, we figured we could make it the rest of the way.

"Guys, it is just too dangerous," William says, countering our ideological ambition with hard realism. "The men who drive those *matatus,* they all have guns. There are many bandits where you must pass through. You white boys from Canada, you will not make it. Even if we went together, I could not protect you."

I look over at Josh. He isn't quite convinced, and William could see that, so he continues. "In my place, in Aweil and around there, everyone has met me. They know who I am; they know my face, my voice. And around Wau, people have heard my name; they know about Captain Kolong. But around Rumbek and those other places...well, I wouldn't go there unless I was ready to fight." He pauses. "And I'm not ready to fight for you guys, okay?" He breaks out in laughter and grabs my shoulder. "What would your dad say if I let you get shot, right here in my country, when you are just visiting from Canada? You come here and—boom!—you are dead. He would be so mad at me!"

Josh and I look at each other. William is right. It would be madness on our part to attempt it. But worse still, it would put William in a situation where he feels responsible for our safety. And for us to take that risk would be unfair to him.

We sit in silence. Then William pipes up.

"So here's what we can do," he says. "We can send the bike mill on the *matatu,* strapped on the roof. That way you can accomplish your goal, and I can keep you safe at the same time." Josh and I decide this is an entirely reasonable idea. "Give me the money we need to pay the transport costs for the bike mill," William says, "and I will organize to have it loaded on tomorrow morning. If you try to negotiate with them, the price will be too high."

"Okay," I say to William. "But how will we get from Juba to Aweil?"

"Ah, boys," he replies. "You will see."

7

High Above the Bandits

The Russian Mi-8T helicopter was built to carry troops and heavy artillery. But the one I'm strapped into now doesn't carry weapons of war anymore. Instead of transporting soldiers to the front lines, this Soviet-era chopper flies United Nations humanitarian workers to their own battlefield: the farthest reaches of South Sudan. And today, we're joining them on board.

As the engines fire up and the blades begin to rotate, the body of the helicopter starts bouncing. I peer out the porthole windows and watch the shadows spin faster and faster, until they blur into a black circle set against the red-earth runway. It's deafeningly loud, even with the ear protector headset on. The safety instructions are written in Cyrillic, but the co-pilot gives us the run-down in simple English: keep seatbelt on, no photos, no smoking. Then he plugs in his headset and gives us the thumbs-up. Ready for takeoff.

Airplanes roll down runways and helicopters lift straight up, right? That's what I thought, but this flying machine does a combination of both.

After several minutes of sitting stationary, the blades spinning furiously, we ease forward and start rolling along the airstrip like we are in a plane and it's business as usual. Then suddenly, we lift straight up, and within minutes we are thousands of metres above Northern Bahr el Ghazal State.

The Mi-8T was designed to move heavy payloads; in combat it

could load four tonnes of military supplies. Today there are no mu-nitions and no armaments aboard, only about twenty passengers—three of whom are Josh, William and me—and stacks of luggage strapped down with rope netting. The co-pilot catches my attention and instructs me to open the window behind. This is not normally something you are allowed to do in an aircraft, so I take full advan-tage. I open the window by lifting it inward and latching it above my head, then reposition my body, crane my neck out the window and close my eyes. I'm sure it looks silly, but it feels utterly amazing. It's like being a kid on a swing and finding that magical place on the arc—that spot between the upswing and the downswing, where you are perfectly suspended, almost floating, and it feels like time just stops.

"While you're looking out there," William jokes, "be sure to check for incoming missiles." I turn my head to look at him. "A year ago," he continues, "one of these UN helicopters was shot down." I have second thoughts about the window, but then realize the ab-surdity of it. If the helicopter were to be hit by a missile, it wouldn't matter if I was leaning out the window or not.

I look over at Josh. His window doesn't open, so he's not get-ting the exposure factor, but he still looks pretty impressed that we are travelling by helicopter. He notices me noticing him, and he reaches over, slaps my thigh and says something I can't make out. But it doesn't matter, because I know exactly what he's thinking. It's what I'm thinking, too.

The Flour Peddler has been in my thoughts, in one form or an-other, for the past six years. But never in a million years would I have seen this coming. Here we are, on the penultimate leg of our journey to Panlang—a staggering 16,245 kilometres from the grain shack in Roberts Creek—flying in a Russian ex-military chopper alongside UN personnel. And somewhere down below, along that rutted-out road, strapped to the roof of a *matatu* transport van, the bike mill is coming.

A wave of excitement washes over me—an excitement I want to share, so I look over at William. His eyes meet mine, and he smiles. He switches his iPhone to the "selfie" setting, leans over, puts his face next to mine and clicks the shutter.

Thousands of metres below, the earth is burning, the smoke rising in billowing black clouds. Farmers are burning the scrubland to ready the land for grazing cattle. The country unfolding below appears dry, bleak and inhospitable. I turn towards William and yell over the noise of the helicopter. "You walked across this?" He can't hear me, so I point at him, then use my two fingers to mimic legs walking. He understands, nods slowly. I shake my head in disbelief.

William was ten years old when he first heard about the killings in Marial Bai. Raiders, they said. Arabs from the North, on horses, attacked them, killing their men, stealing their daughters, taking their animals. They left, but they would be back. Parents anxiously discussed the dangers, imagined the possible violence. Worried that the boys would be considered potential combatants, the decision was made to send them away. Other villages were doing the same, and it would be safer for them to travel together. Boys were told to go to the house of the paramount chief, who would organize to connect them to the large group that was leaving soon. William said hurried goodbyes, snatched a too-short embrace from his mother, and then he was off—with only the clothes on his back.

He had no idea how long it would take or if he would ever return home.

He was right to wonder. For many boys, this was in fact the last time they would see their families. That night, the boys of Marial Bai headed east, towards Ethiopia. But no one knew how far it was to this place called Ethiopia. It was just over the ridge or it was just another day or just another few days. There was food at the next village or maybe farther ahead at the next one. There was supposed to be water there, or maybe tomorrow at the river, if there was a river.

Days turned to weeks. Sometimes they walked under a blazing sun, sometimes under moonlight. After a while, no one asked how much farther; they just walked. Boys started dropping. Weakened by hunger and thirst, they died in the thousands—brothers, cousins, friends—their bodies leaving a trail of death across Sudan. Those that made it to refugee camps across the border were called the "Lost Boys" by UN workers, a name that stuck—a name that South Sudanese men like William are proud to call themselves.

Staring down from up here, it seems impossible. How could anyone—let alone a young boy—possibly survive? It is painful to think about, but I can't help wondering: would my son have made it? Walking for weeks or months without food, water, clothing or protection? Could Solomon have been a William—or would he lie dead on the earth below me, along with thousands of other sons?

I try to imagine the last goodbye, how I would hold my son tight in my arms, knowing it may be the last time I'd ever see him again. I feel incredibly sad at the magnitude of their loss. Then I feel anger welling up inside me, anger that boys should have to walk for months and see their friends die beside them. Anger that young girls would be captured, raped, impregnated and destined to a life of servitude. Anger that violence would rip families apart and leave death and destruction ...

"Mister!" The Russian co-pilot is trying to get my attention. I snap out of my thoughts, nod that I've seen him. He mimes closing the window, but it takes me a second to realize what he wants. I reach up, click the latch and lower the glass slowly as the chopper descends.

The minibus, the United Nations vehicle that had been waiting at the edge of the Aweil airfield, drives down a straight dirt road, kicking up dust. We pass simple shelters made of tree branches and woven grasses, some with plastic sheeting draped over the roofs. Tall, thin women walk balancing jerry cans on their heads; kids with ragged T-shirts and no pants wander between huts.

We bump onto a raised roadbed, and William gestures behind us. "That is the way to Marial Bai and Panlang, where we will do the bike-mill workshop with the ladies on Sunday. It is sixty kilometres from here, but because the road is bad, it will take us several hours. The way we are headed now is to Aweil town."

The minibus turns onto a strip of blacktop pavement, then whizzes along until we stop at the blue gates of the main UN compound. Guards move along the side of the vehicle, inspecting it, and then the gates swing open. We drive inside onto packed dirt until we come to a stop under the shade of a large tree. The engine cuts out, and the luggage is unloaded, the pile leaning against the tree. William had left his pickup truck here, so we grab our bags and start to hoist them over our shoulders, ready to load up, but he tells us to leave them. "We will go and register first. Don't worry," he adds with a laugh, "no one will take anything."

We follow him along a path, shaded by tall broad-leafed trees, towards a cluster of portable buildings. We step up onto a cement sidewalk, which runs diagonally through the compound and connects the various portable buildings. In an otherwise rustic compound like this, the only purpose I can think of for such an expensive sidewalk would be to keep the shoes of visiting diplomats clean. Birds twitter in the branches above as we pass one portable, then turn to enter another. We follow William inside and exchange pleasantries with the man at the desk, who hands us some forms to fill out.

Having inherited the last name Hergesheimer, I've been resigned to spelling it for several decades. Unsurprisingly, it took me longer to learn how to print my name than my classmates who were born into families with simple surnames like Smith or Jones. For a Hergesheimer, filling out forms is pretty much our rite of passage, a way of demonstrating allegiance and/or acknowledgement of our (faded) German heritage. It's especially tedious when the form requires you to print block capitals into little boxes (whoever invented that, thanks a lot, signed: a man with thirty-three letters in his name). If I had a nickel for every time I had leftover letters dangling in the right-hand margin, I'd be rich.

I lean over the page and start in: C H R I S T O P H E R P A T R I C K H E R G E S H E I M E R.

I hear William's infectious laugh fill the room, but I stay focused on the form. I fish out my passport and start transferring the information. It's always some variation on the same information: name, country of citizenship, passport number, date, place of issue. I wonder if UN workers have all their details memorized, having to fill out an endless array of forms. Josh is trying to keep a conversation going with the man behind the desk, but I'm anxious to get moving, and I get distracted and have to return to a section I missed.

The man at the desk is from Toronto. He introduced himself earlier, but I can't remember his name. He tells us he's heading home for the Christmas holidays, via Juba and Entebbe, on KLM through Amsterdam. In fact, we're scheduled to be on the helicopter back to Juba with him in four days.

"You guys sure have a good connection with William," the man behind the desk says. "He got you UN clearance on the chopper, both directions."

William gives us a look, as if to say "See, you won't need those airline tickets we bought in Juba after all."

The man behind the desk informs us about the logistics: the UN flight manifest isn't set until forty-eight hours before departure, but our names had been registered early, and that was normally the most important thing. "Of course, if for some reason a whole bunch of bigwigs want to fly back to Juba on that day," he says, "you'll be out of luck. But that's pretty unlikely."

The forms complete, we shake hands and head out, walking back to the large tree where our bags sit in the shade, undisturbed. "See?" William says. "I told you, this is a safe place."

Josh and I heave our bags into the back of William's pick-up truck. Before he takes us to the UN's World Food Programme (WFP) compound, where we will be staying, we are going to meet his family. Josh and I both want to ride in the bed of the truck. William tells us there is space in the cab, but we climb in the back and sit down. William shrugs and climbs in the driver's seat, while Josh gets out his camera, ready to snap photos. At the gate, one guard says something to William. William gets out and walks back to explain to us. "This guy is saying, 'Why do you make the white men ride in the back? What is wrong with you that you treat them this way?' I tried to tell him you want to ride in the back, but he doesn't believe me. He is asking why a white man who is so rich and important would want to ride like a poor man, exposed to the heat and the dust? I told him you guys like to travel the local way. He said he has never encountered white men thinking like this before." We understand and flash the guard a thumbs-up sign, and he waves us through.

The truck turns onto a gravel road, and the housing changes: squat brick buildings with corrugated metal roofs, plaster and cement structures inside compound walls. This section of Aweil is more demarcated, more permanent. We pass a group of boys playing a ball game in the road. The boys notice Josh and me riding in the back of the truck, exchange looks with one another, then sprint after the truck, yelling, calling more boys as they go. More join the running group, and by the time we arrive at William's home, at least a dozen have gathered.

We pull up in front of a long metal gate, and William hops out. "Boys," he says with pride, keys rattling as the gate swings open, "welcome to my home." We stand up in the back of the truck and ready ourselves to start unloading our bags for safekeeping. The group of boys shout and point at us, coming closer, but then hang back, unsure of how we will respond. I hop down and Josh begins tossing me the bags. The cluster of boys watch; several of them inch closer. I look over my shoulder, and they smile and point. I start towards them, but they retreat, regrouping farther down the road near a drainage ditch. I jog a bit towards them, and they break out laughing and scatter. I laugh too; then I head back to the truck, shoulder my bag and go inside.

But before we head to the WFP compound, where we will spend the night, we will meet some of William's friends.

The Aweil Grand Hotel is far from grand, a three-storey concrete box surrounded by piles of gravel and pits dug by hand. But the political movers and shakers of Northern Bahr el Ghazal don't seem to mind. William introduces them around the plastic table: Minister of Education, Minister of Health, Minister of the interior. Each man has two smartphones—iPhones and Nokias purchased abroad—and they laugh at Josh's old Samsung and tell us to sit down and order a beer. Once again, I'm the lone Bell in a sea of Tuskers.

The men stop talking during the hourly news broadcast that crackles through a cellphone speaker. The news is full of updates on government negotiations taking place in Juba. According to reports, Vice-President Riek Machar has pulled out of negotiations aimed at resolving the political conflict that has been brewing since President Salva Kiir Mayardit dismissed his entire cabinet in July. The parties are still far apart in the negotiations process, but they hope to resume talks tomorrow.

There is some minor discussion about South Sudanese politics, and then the conversation switches—to us, to Canada, to our bike-mill project. After hearing that I study at UBC, one of the men says,

"I too studied at UBC, years ago." Then he leans across the table, like he's confiding in me. "Do you know what happens if you are even the slightest bit late paying your student fees?"

I'm not sure what to say in response, so I just shrug.

"I don't either!" He slaps the table. "I studied on a government bursary—when Khartoum was paying the bill—and somehow, even having received my degree, I found that I still owe four hundred dollars."

I shrug again. Perhaps he is worried I will be offended that he owes my alma mater money.

"Do you think they will try to make me pay this amount?" he asks, with an air of seriousness. "It was not a problem of my own making, after all."

A man wearing suit slacks and a Saskatchewan Roughriders jersey pipes up. "Perhaps they will sell your debt to a collection agency," he muses. I can't tell if he's joking or not, so I hold back a laugh. "And then," he says, "we can expect a letter to arrive on the UN helicopter which reads 'Dear minister of such-and-such, Aweil, South Sudan, it appears your account is in arrears.'"

The men break out laughing. I speculate that the worst UBC could do would be to withhold his academic transcripts, and then I offer to ask on his behalf when I get back to UBC. "No," he wags his finger. "Say only that it is a 'someone' who is asking, like in hypothetical terms. And do not divulge my specific location."

The sun is setting now, the last band of yellow in the west being chased out by the eastern darkness. We climb in the truck and drive for a few minutes, then pull up next to a compound with large metal doors.

Inside, the music is thumping and the generator is roaring as it powers the main nightclub in Aweil. The floor is packed dirt and the tables are plastic patio furniture, but there is plenty of cold beer and goat meat grilling over an oil-drum barbeque, charcoal embers glowing red. We join a table of twelve, all males. This is definitely the kind of place Josh and I would never come to if we weren't William's guests, and realizing he's watching out for us made me feel safe—safe enough to have another beer, at least.

There's a DJ booth set up in the corner and a projector screen, which displays a pirated mash-up of the best West African, Caribbean and American music videos—oiled and nearly naked women, gyrating hips and thrusting pelvises beside men wearing gold necklaces and brandishing expensive cellphones. It is possibly one of the most intriguing and disconcerting aspects of globalization. By the third round of beers, however, any lingering concerns I have about the negative impacts of the crass commercialism and overt sexuality can only be met by trying to ignore the screen and just enjoy the thumping music.

One of the guys at our table shouts over the music, "If you drink Heineken, you must order two!" He's slurring his words and letting his head flop around while speaking. "Each can is smaller, you see." He waves the can, explaining how important it is to keep pace with your drinking mates. He's had ten beers so far, "but only ordered five rounds!" he exclaims, validating the theory. He tries to goad me into a drinking match, but I say I need to go the bathroom and get up.

The toilet is a closet-sized cement box in the corner of the yard. There is no light bulb inside, and it stinks so badly I can't get close to the entrance. A guy from our table pushes past me, stands at the door and pisses into the darkness. He laughs, zips up and staggers back towards the music. I feel bad for whoever is going to have to clean this, but I really do have to go, so I let it rip from the door as well.

"That place is too rowdy!" William says as we walk out the gate. "Tomorrow we can drink a beer back at the UN compound, where we can sit with politicians and development workers. That is a better place for us. At this place, the people can get too excited, and bad things happen sometimes."

That night we go to sleep intoxicated and exhausted, but utterly pleased with ourselves. From here on out, it would be clear sailing. Drive to Panlang, hand over the bike mill, do the workshop, then it was over. We had made it.

Josh wakes me the next morning with news of the shootings in Juba. There were reports that hundreds were killed, with bodies in the streets, and thousands of civilians were seeking shelter in UN compounds across the country. President Salva Kiir Mayardit announced there had been an attempted coup, and he imposed immediate security measures: a curfew had been issued and the airport was closed indefinitely.

Suddenly, getting home for Christmas became a lot more complicated.

Opposite: Chris demonstrating the flour mill to his son, Sol.
Photo Christina Symons.

Above: Chris in full action on the bike mill in Vancouver.

Oposite top: The early Flour Peddler booth (with Amanda-Rae in the background) at the Powell River Local Grain Day in 2008.

Opposite bottom: The bike mill producing freshly ground spelt flour.

Above: Christopher (left), the manager of the welding shop at the Juba Technical School, welds a bicycle sprocket onto the flywheel of the grain mill in preparation for the trip to Panlang.

Opposite: Chris in front of the gate to the Juba Technical School.

Above: A cattle herder drives his herd along the road.

Opposite top: A roadside shop in Juba.

Opposite bottom: A woman in Juba prepares a fried egg and chapatti roll.

Above: Chris on the road to the Juba Technical School.

Opposite top: Headmaster John Manas (left), Josh (centre) and Christopher, the welding shop manager at the Juba Technical school.

Opposite bottom: A boy returning home after filling a water jug at the Nile river in Terekeka, fifty kilometres from Juba. The Pan Aweil Development Agency started a biosand water filter project, so the villagers could access safe drinking water.

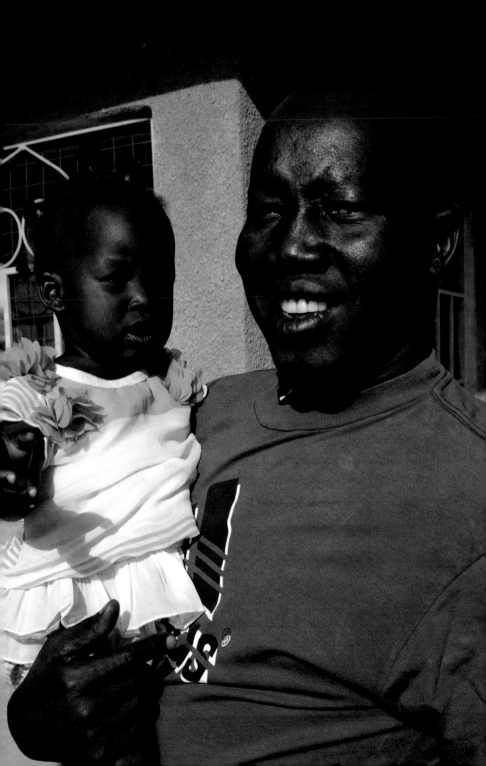

Above: A villager rests in the afternoon sun in one of the settlements around Aweil.

Opposite: William Kolong at home in Aweil with his daughter Aweki.

Following pages: The children who live around the World Food Programme compound in Aweil ham it up for the camera.

Pages 158-159: Chris and William conducting a bike-mill workshop for the Panlang women's cooperative.

Page 160: The children of Panlang were fascinated by the bike mill.

Part III

Country Living

AWEIL DEVELOPMENT AGENCY

8

Trials and Tribulations

The Flour Peddler perimeter had been breached sometime in the early morning hours of October 22, 2010, while I lay sleeping. The grain shack lock-up isn't exactly Fort Knox, but so far it has been sufficient to keep the creatures of the forest at bay. The red door is swinging, ripped open by brute force and animal instinct. I notice the claw marks, turn back to the house, and mouth the word "bear" to Amanda-Rae, who is watching from the window. Then I walk among the carnage, picking my way through grain strewn in front of the door. Strips of ripped paper bag tell a story of success, an animal reaping the rewards of its labour. He came, he smelled, he conquered—leaving with a full belly and leaving us the bill, as well as piles of steaming scat in the driveway, the undigested kernels evidence for a charge of grain larceny.

As I move closer to survey the interior damage, A-Rae calls out from the house, "Is the bear gone?" I have been operating under that assumption, but have no visual confirmation. "You should check before you go inside," she adds.

If the bear was still inside, I probably would have seen it by now. Still, point taken. I step inside and crunch across the layer of grain carpeting the entryway. Lids pried off, bins tipped over and raided. A quick inventory reveals I've lost sixty kilograms of kernels.

The Pan Aweil Development Agency bike mill was received with enthusiasm and curiosity in Panlang.

Instinct tells me to scrape some up, skim off some for my family at least—but common sense and echoes of that food safety course I took two years ago hold me back.

I walk to the side of the house and down the hill to check on the chickens. I half-anticipate slaughter, but I find them still puffed up on their perches, their feathers inflated against the chill of late October. I don't sense fear when I look into their beady eyes, so I figure the bear must have missed them. Then I turn and walk back up the hill to face the grain shack catastrophe.

I thought the Flour Peddler had hit rock bottom that day. Once again, I look on the bright side: Good thing it's the end of market season; I've got time to regroup before spring.

But then, just before the first summer markets of 2011 commenced, things got even worse.

"The van doesn't shift into reverse anymore," I told Amanda-Rae one evening.

"Hmmm..." she half-answered, stirring the stewing lentils.

Some spouses would be surprised by the revelation that the family vehicle wasn't operating properly. Amanda-Rae was not, which is probably part of why we are married. She tapped the spoon on the edge of the pot and said, "How's that going to work at the market, you know, unloading?" I shrugged. She laughed a bit, then tasted the lentils. "I'd love to see the guy next to you as you do a wide-ass circumference pull-in," she said. I can always count on her for support during trying times, which is probably another reason why we are married.

It is Saturday, June 19, 2011, the height of market season. I've already finalized sixteen market bookings, so cancelling is out of the question. Unfortunately, I've depleted our bank account with an advance purchase of four hundred kilograms of grain, so paying to repair the vehicle is out of the question. And this leaves me with no option but to move forward, literally, with my hobbled vehicle.

After all, five out of six gears still work, which in the social sciences is a pretty strong statistic.

Having done a realistic assessment of my turning radius, I wisely elect to park outside the lot and use my daughter's wagon to carry my pop-up tent, table, bike mill and six bins of flour to my stall. But first, I must find that elusive parking spot that I can get into—and out of—without backing up. Closest to the intersection would be best, but today it is unavailable. I park three blocks away, which gives me plenty of time to ponder my situation as I fight to keep the wagon from tipping over. Obviously, this wagon isn't meant for children intending to run a farmers' market business. But it's okay, I tell myself. I spin it like a business slogan. "The Flour Peddler doesn't have a reverse gear!" I joke to neighbouring stallholders, who watch me make five trips back to my vehicle— several blocks away—with a mixture of fascination and pity.

It's 8:05 a.m. After unloading the wagon for the fifth time, I can now start setting up my booth. By now, I've sort of given up on the bike mill. It was great in the beginning, but the pieces don't fit together properly and the belt is twisted like a knot in a kid's hair. Once a performance tool, it is now for display purposes only. If anyone asks me about it, I use the usual "technical issue" excuse and successfully "reflect and redirect" the conversation.

Let's move on to the tent—a standard ten-by-ten-foot pop-up variety. If there's anything I've learned over the years, it's that with market tents, you get what you pay for. A trusted name-brand tent will be sturdy, lasting for many seasons with proper care and maintenance. To ensure maximum lifespan, one should always perform set-up and take-down carefully, ideally with a partner who can co-ordinate the raising and lowering to ensure nothing gets bent. And one should always pack the tent back inside its carrying case. I never did any of these things, and thus went through three tents in four years of operation.

Above my head, you'll find my sign hanging over the table. It's true: a good sign speaks volumes about the business. When I started this business, I always imagined I'd be a roll-up vinyl sign kind of guy. But it never worked out. Instead, the night before my first Trout Lake market, I scavenged a piece of wood siding five feet long and nine inches wide, and had my wife paint THE FLOUR PEDDLER on it. I found a half-used roll of twine in the garden shed and loaded both in the van. At the market, I realized I had neglected to drill holes in the ends, so instead of the sign hanging confidently above my table, it rested tenuously inside large loops of twine hung from the crossbars. While attempting to hoist it up, I also realized the sign weighed close to fifteen pounds, making it a potential hazard to customers below. But having already invested time and energy in this sign, I wasn't about to abandon it for something unknown—better the devil you know, I believe the saying goes. So I resolved to drill holes in the sign immediately upon returning home, which I actually did that night, confirming to myself that I was becoming more organized. Late at night, however, after my family was sound asleep, I entertained impure thoughts about roll-up vinyl signs, advertising my sophistication like the neon lights of Times Square or the Las Vegas Strip.

But never mind all that. Now it's 8:47 a.m. and I'm around the corner in the bushes by the lakeshore, shovelling dirt with a piece of cedar siding, trying to fill empty grain bags. Not for sale, of course—for weight. There are only thirteen minutes until the market opens for business, and so far, none of the staff have noticed that I don't have any tent weights. I have a few broken bricks I collected from Josh's place earlier this morning, but not forty pounds' worth. Infractions result in a "tent weight fine" of twenty dollars— almost half the cost of the market fee. Doesn't sound like much, but it adds up. I have already used up my "weight credit" with the stallholders beside me (a technique that consists of pleading with neighbouring vendors to strap their weights across our touching tent legs), hence the dirt-filled bags.

Entrepreneurs who want to get into the farmers' market business need to invest in the infrastructure. The tent is obvious, ditto the table. But there are also plenty of small but significant items vendors require that are a mystery to the uninitiated: for example, tent weights times four. Those with foresight and disposable income buy purpose-made tent weights, canvas bags weighing precisely ten pounds (4.5 kgs) that wrap around the tent legs and secure with Velcro. The creative types save money by pouring sand into milk jugs or filling PVC pipe-ends with cement. The common theme is, of course, the investment of money, time or effort that results in something that meets the criteria. I'm in the "dirt bag" category, which works, but definitely leads to an unappetizing display when the bags on the table have the same label as the tent weights behind you.

I never did sort out the tent weights. Not that I didn't know better; I've watched four-hundred-dollar tents blow away or bend beyond repair, not to mention the risks they posed to other vendors and unsuspecting shoppers during a strong wind. Many mornings I'd grumble as I scanned the parking lot for small boulders, but by the afternoon, as I was cruising back to the ferry terminal, all thoughts of organizing something weighted before the next market would have disappeared, pushed out by a more immediate concern: raiding the float for enough change for my ferry ticket home.

You know what they say: a good market vendor needs a well-stocked float like an electrician needs pliers and a carpenter needs a tape measure. Well, let's just say it's a good thing I'm not in either of those trades. My market float generally consisted of the change from a BC Ferries coffee, a crumpled ten-dollar bill fished from a back pocket and whatever change I could scrounge from the dashboard cup holders. Sometimes I sprinted to Safeway or the local gas station at 8:40 a.m. to buy single granola bars (which then became the day's lunch) in order to break twenty-dollar bills to supplement my insufficient coinage.

I did everything except ask other vendors for change.

It's the unspoken market rule that you don't ask another stallholder to top up your float, which is comparable perhaps to pumping iron in the prison yard out of turn. And although you're unlikely to get shanked by the artisan soap maker, violating this market protocol comes with lasting social consequences. Earning a reputation as "that guy who never has any change" is the equivalent of donning the scarlet letter or flying the flag of Black Death from your stall. Soon other vendors avoid meeting your gaze and rustle around inside boxes as you approach, ensuring they appear too busy to offer assistance.

There are plenty of vendors who have a dedicated box in which they maintain a favourable amount of change and bills. Let's just call these vendors "organized," for simplicity's sake. I would watch the "organized" from afar and ponder the applicability of the biblical commandment regarding coveting thy neighbour's ox. How I lusted after their succulent spread of five-, ten- and twenty-dollar bills, which burst with colour like a painter's palette! The way their metal float boxes would jingle as they were unloaded like a symphony of quarters, dimes and nickels, each coin providing a unique voice in their own dedicated section of the orchestra.

The "organized" maintain their float similarly to the way fastidious people trim their hedges, which is to say, very properly. At the close of business, the organized would remove the day's earnings and assess the float. If depleted, they would endeavour to replenish the supply with a visit to a financial institution to convert bills to coins, ensuring their readiness for the upcoming week.

In contrast, I've funded many a ferry ticket with toonies, bought groceries with loonies and quarters, and stacked enough dimes for the occasional tequila shot, an activity that also functions as a sobriety test. As I always say—and not just when inebriated—money is money, and dimes are as much a legitimate currency as a fifty-dollar bill.

To say I pilfered my float each week would be inaccurate, as pilfering implies taking some but leaving enough so as not to attract attention. It would be more accurate to say I pillaged the float the way warriors raiding a medieval fortress would, leaving overturned goblets and torn tapestries in their wake. However, with a nod to my better nature, I did try to ensure there were some coins in the van's cup holder for next week.

When I tell people these types of stories, it's easy for them to write me off as a guy who should not have been in business in the first place. Easy to say, because it's true. I'm a sociologist, remember? I started the Flour Peddler because I loved milling my own grain and baking kickass muffins, not because I was savvy enough to sense a niche in the market and fill it in the most profitable manner. For me, it was about forming a 100 percent southwestern BC grain chain, and educating people about that grain chain. It was never because I wanted to be a "businessman" or because I loved marketing.

But that's the funny thing about business. Once you've been running a business for a few years, you come to the cold realization that your business isn't just about the product, that thing you're selling because you are passionate about it. It's about running a business.

Like a monk struck by an epiphany while pondering the meaning of existence on a lofty mountaintop, I woke one morning in a cold sweat to a cruel realization: loving your product and the philosophy behind it, believing in it with all your heart and pouring all your energy and more into it is not enough. You can't force your business to succeed this way. You actually have to be good at managing it. And that's a hard truth to accept.

I admit I'm not the most organized person. Ask anyone who knows me, and they would be more than happy to tell you how they've witnessed my inefficiency firsthand. In fact, most people would tell you that they are surprised my business lasted as long as it did.

It's not like I didn't work hard. I put in thousands of hours. But it didn't help.

Business gurus will tell you the goal is always to "work smarter, not harder." But with milling, I couldn't really speed up the production without some significant investments and restructuring. I had an eight-inch stone mill that took four minutes to grind a kilogram. Once I measured out the grain and poured it into the hopper, it wasn't really "work," per se, as I didn't have to do anything. But four minutes isn't long enough to do much else except press a label on a bag, insert the funnel scoop into the top of the bag and get the other scoop ready.

When Jules was on the payroll, she made the most of those four minutes. She would take a sip of red wine and flip through a magazine, or stop to watch a bird digging for worms outside the grain shed. But when I was grinding, I was on a mission. Actually, I was on four missions simultaneously: mentally writing my master's dissertation; checking outside to ensure my children hadn't injured themselves; typing a text to the bass player of my band; and skimming a lengthy email from a lady in Nova Scotia who had heard about the Flour Peddler and wanted a recipe. When the pitch of the grinder changed, indicating the last kernels had flowed through, I would stop, mid-email, to put the flour in the bag and seal the top. Then I would scoop raw kernels out of a bag, measure them on the scale, pour them into the hopper—and it was déjà vu.

Saturday is market day at Trout Lake in Vancouver—9:00 a.m. to 2:00 p.m. But the preparations begin early Friday morning. Here's a standard play-by-play:

Friday

7:02 a.m. Attempt to continue sleeping off late-night shenanigans while toddlers demand attention. Flour Peddler pancakes and coffee for breakfast.

9:12 a.m. Open door of grain shed, open sack of grain, calibrate scale.

9:14 a.m. Weigh one kilo of whole grain on scale. Turn on stone mill and empty contents of scale into mill. Wait requisite four minutes. Use metal scoop to empty flour drawer into bag. Seal bag and affix label.

9:18 a.m. Put bag in flour bin for transport. One down.

9:19 a.m. Make thirty-nine more bags.

1:23 p.m. Eat lunch.

1:52 p.m. Make thirty-seven more bags.

4:26 p.m. Clean grain shack.

5:08 p.m. Load van.

5:52 p.m. Eat dinner with family.

7:02 p.m. Relax, knowing all preparations are complete.

8:42 p.m. Mild paranoia sets in. Return to grain shack.

8:43 p.m. Make seventeen additional bags.

10:07 p.m. Clean up again.

10:17 p.m. Milling done.

10:18 p.m. Pour glass of wine and sit on porch.

11:22 p.m. Pour remainder of bottle into glass.

Saturday

1:47 a.m. Wake up paranoid about missing the ferry.

2:12 a.m. Wake up when kids find their way into our bed.

3:19 a.m. Wake up feeling paranoid, exhausted and frustrated.

4:42 a.m. Alarm clock blares. Snooze button.

5:10 a.m. Alarm clock blares again. Snooze button.

5:19 a.m. Brush teeth. Splash face with water.

5:21 a.m. Coffee number one.

5:31 a.m. Leave for ferry.

5:46 a.m. Coffee number two.

5:57 a.m. Arrive at Langdale ferry terminal. Fall asleep in van.

6:07 a.m. Wake up to cars being loaded.

6:18 a.m. Coffee number three onboard at BC Ferries café.

6:22 a.m. Stare blankly out window, consider sleeping.

7:00 a.m. Dock at Horseshoe Bay and start driving.

7:37 a.m. Coffee number four. Realize this is already way too many coffees.

7:42 a.m. Arrive at Trout Lake parking lot in East Vancouver.

7:46 a.m. Find stall number and begin unloading.

7:47 a.m. Realize I forgot market tent weights. Again.

7:55 a.m. Unload and build market stall. Assess state of market float.

8:27 a.m. Walk aimlessly (use getting coffee as a tangible goal), watching others set up. Offer tired waves, salutes or good mornings.

9:00 a.m. Bell rings; market begins.

9:01 a.m. to 1:59 p.m. Sell flour!

2:00 p.m. Bell rings; market closes. Walk to van and wait to be allowed to drive inside to load.

2:20 p.m. Load furiously; speed is everything.

2:33 p.m. Leave for ferry. Attempt to make the 3:30 p.m. sailing.

Preferred outcome: Make the 3:30 p.m. sailing. Try to sleep in a seat that cannot recline. Try not to look in the rear-view mirror at the jumble of market infrastructure piled haphazardly behind the seat like a shipwreck.

Actual outcome: Miss the 3:30 p.m. sailing and go into Horseshoe Bay to eat fish and chips while awaiting the 5:30 p.m. sailing. Order a beer after news that ferry is delayed. Cost of less-preferred outcome: twenty-four dollars.

7:05 p.m. Dock at Langdale. Contemplate the meaning of capitalism while sitting behind a large truck that is towing a glossy speedboat. Feel personally offended when other rows of vehicles off-load first.

7:25 p.m. Turn off on Day Road. Try not to race up the driveway.

7:26 p.m. Kiss kids and lovely wife.

7:27 p.m. Open beer on porch. Resist urge to count money, revel in success.

7:28 p.m. Break down and open cash box. Feel the rush of the first beer. Count bills slowly, then spread them like a fan. Ponder what it feels like to work at a money exchange booth.

7:44 p.m. Count every coin, even the ones you are sure were in the float from last week. Try to guess artificially inflated total.

7:59 p.m. Determine total weekend's profit is $186. Open another beer.

9

A Grain-Chain Community

I was always amazed at the tenacity of farmers' market shoppers. They appeared as apparitions in rain, sleet, hail and wind, clad in wet weather gear.

At first glance, it doesn't make sense for someone to deliberately shop outside, at least not when the weather is hideous. But you don't have to be a sociologist to recognize that a farmers' market is about more than just fresh produce; it's a grassroots method for fostering relationships over food that has been around in one form or another for thousands of years.

The people who bought from the Flour Peddler could easily purchase flour somewhere else—somewhere warm and dry, at the very least—but they made the effort to buy my flour because we had built a relationship. Sure, economics were involved: they got fresh flour and I got some cash. But we also had a history. Over the years, we connected as they watched my business grow and evolve. We weren't friends, but we were mutual providers. I don't want to over-romanticize it, but the customers were a big part of why I kept at it through those years.

It was the Polish lady who loved the oats I flaked by hand, but hated the plastic Ziploc bag I packed them in. It was the awestruck parents recounting tales of their otherwise picky children ravenously attacking whole-wheat muffins. It was the sourdough enthusiast who was constantly re-evaluating her baking recipes, returning each time with a smile and an anecdote. The validation and acknowledgement I received was usually enough to keep my spirits up, even as the rain came down.

When I explained how important the customers were to me, people would often reply, "Well, every business owner gets satisfaction from serving their customers." To that, I would always answer that the Flour Peddler wasn't just about selling bags of flour to farmers' market shoppers; the Flour Peddler was about networking through food processing, and connecting people from across southwestern BC.

The North Okanagan holds a special place in my heart, because it's managed to preserve some of its traditional—and now much less profitable—industries. In the last few decades, the South Okanagan has been colonized by wine enthusiasts converting orchards to vineyards, and enticing visitors to spa weekends at luxury hotels with deep-blue swimming pools and tastefully decorated tasting rooms. So I always enjoyed heading to the Fieldstone Organics Granary, the grain depot just outside of Armstrong in the North Okanagan where I bought the majority of my wheat stock each autumn, and then in smaller lots throughout the year. The hills on either side are brown and green, the valley floor is carpeted in glorious gold, the scent of cow manure fills the air and the smell of cheese wafts on the breeze.

What began a decade ago as a farmer-led co-operative has now flowered into one of our province's gems. Fieldstone prides itself on being BC's only certified-organic grain handling facility, which was precisely what I needed, because 90 percent of my farmers' market customers were looking for organic and only organic. What's more, Fieldstone is the only place in southwestern BC where I could purchase specialty grains like spelt, rye and oats. Over the years, I also purchased bags of emmer and Khorasan wheat (the official, untrademarked name for Kamut), ancient varieties I sourced after customers asked me about these grains, which I hadn't been able to find anywhere local before.

The Fieldstone Granary sources their crops from nearby farms, so they always had enough to fill my orders. I think they did it partly because I was a solid repeat customer (though I sometimes carried a few payments in arrears), but mostly because they supported my vision: sharing interior BC grain with customers in the province's southwestern corner. Though it is still a co-operative at heart, Fieldstone is no small-potatoes operation, and it is known throughout the region as the only place with the machine required to hull grains. The folks at Fieldstone sell to millers, bakers and retailers far and wide, but they always kept enough for my order aside, just to ensure I got mine when I needed it.

The Okanagan wins hands-down for its vibrant colours and the striking contrasts between its deep-green valley floor, its sparkling lakes and the brown hills that keep it hemmed in on both sides. But it's at the shore of the Pacific Ocean, where waves crash against the edge of Sea Bluff Farm in Metchosin on Vancouver Island, that I feel the strongest connection to the terrain.

Sea Bluff Farm is where Tom Henry sold me my first batch of red fife, a few weeks after I met him at the Bread and Wheat Festival in Victoria. I continued to buy some other hard red spring varieties from Tom for several seasons, and we formed a solid relationship. I swore I could taste the touch of salt that had lingered near his fields as the ocean spray evaporated in the coastal air.

But I will never forget the kernels that got me hooked and started me on this crazy journey: that soft white wheat I bought from Jim Grieshaber-Otto at Cedar Isle Farm in Agassiz. Jim is an academic and a writer, as well as a great farmer and a father of two, and we connected immediately. He became an integral go-to person while I was conducting my research, and his family was always welcoming and supportive of my milling and research endeavours.

But Jim and I weren't only business partners. We also collaborated via the FarmFolk CityFolk connection on a few community projects, most notably the Urban Grains CSA, a Community Supported Agriculture model that delivers raw kernels and flour, which are ground at Anita's Organic Mill in Chilliwack, to more than ninety families living in and around Vancouver. Although I had no role in the milling for this project, I got involved in other ways, helping with the distribution and assisting with the occasional farm tour.

It wasn't only the suppliers who supported my efforts, either. Several skilled artisan bakers and high-end chefs purchased my southwestern BC grain, even though my prices were far from competitive. I sold to Terra Breads in Vancouver, The Sweet Chef Bakery in Gibsons, and many other bakeries and restaurants that featured Flour Peddler products in a variety of baked items, from waffles to cookies to focaccia breads. I even milled and sold for a stretch to a sourdough enthusiast who baked one of the greatest rye loaves and delivered it by bicycle. These bakers were willing to take a chance on me, a small-scale miller, and turn my product into some amazing creations. I'll never forget how beautiful those products looked, how fantastic they tasted, and how proud I felt to be involved.

I like to reflect on the relationships I've cultivated with these growers over the half-decade I've been in business. In the flour milling business, which typically relies on making bulk, seasonal purchases, I wouldn't have been able to operate without the commitment of people like Jim, Tom and the folks at Fieldstone to fill my smaller orders. What they had available, they would sell to me. I was an important outlet for their product, especially for Tom's red fife, which many connoisseurs on the Sunshine Coast came to love. Nurturing these relationships with the growers gave me stability, even if I didn't end up turning a profit that year. But most importantly, they made me proud of what I was selling—a 100 percent southwestern BC grain chain—and what I was doing as a community miller, getting the grains of southwestern BC into the backpacks, cloth bags and bike panniers of the farmers' market shoppers.

The relationships I formed with growers were vital, to be sure, but perhaps no less important than the ones we vendors cultivated with each other. Although not all those relationships were deep, patterns were formed, and we had the knowledge that despite the variation of our products, we shared a common experience. The unspoken understanding we shared when helping another vendor set up a tent was powerful. Like the revolutionary fighter who understands that the group's power comes from the cohesive whole, we understood that the market's foundation was based on our relationships.

And this was even more important when it came to supporting each other in our various commitments—including our families.

The small farmers' market on the Sunshine Coast provided a venue and a supportive community where I could turn my kids loose while I worked.

My kids were never interested in helping with the production process. That would be child labour, after all. But it's safe to say they were part of the vending experience. They contributed by keeping themselves busy at the market while Amanda-Rae and I sold the flour. And this was only possible because of the support system provided by the farmers' market "family"—relationships that I relied on to continue.

Our kids were raised "free range" at the Sechelt Farmers' Market. The thrill of selling flour in the booth was lost on them, so as soon as they could walk, they started to explore. In those days, the market took place in the parking lot of the Ravens Cry theatre/ Tems Swiya museum along Highway 101, a less-than-ideal venue for children still unfamiliar with the dangers of oncoming traffic. The only bathroom was inside the museum, which meant the kids had to walk past interesting looking things that *could never be touched*, especially not the tiny willow bark canoe in the lobby.

My children were not the only free-range children. Ours were the youngest, however, being mentored in the ways of survival by the Oliver Twist-like street urchins of the Sechelt Farmers' Market, begging for baked goods and fresh berries, and dashing in and out of narrow corridors behind vendors, always inches away from sending a potter's stand crashing down like an uncontrolled demolition.

Once the Farm Gate Market in Roberts Creek got going—a market I helped start—the situation for children improved dramatically. The gravel parking lot backed onto a forest behind the Roberts Creek Hall, and soon the ragtag group of children became explorers and conquistadors. As soon as the market set-up began, they would scatter into the forest, emerging a few hours later adorned in fern leaves and brandishing sticks, a motley crew of grass-stained, muddy, hungry—but happy—kids.

There was talk at one point of a craft station, clowns or entertainers, some type of organized children's activities. But these children had been raised to fend for themselves. Who needed a clown when you could swing off the top of a dumpster using the long branches of a cedar tree and land in a pile of moss-covered bricks? Glue sticks and sparkles have temporary appeal, but branches, leaves and rudimentary stone tools were all the art supplies they needed. The more entrepreneurial children started gathering blackberries and digging up licorice ferns to sell. They would wander around the market, looking like customers and chewing on their unwashed product. With all the dirt on their faces, I'd joke that they looked like chimney sweeps, and then pay a quarter to chew on the odd piece of licorice fern, just to keep the business spirit alive and kicking.

The farmers' market was a weekly free-for-all for these children. Unlike me, they never complained about having to go. Their games taught them valuable lessons about how food comes from neighbours, hard work and conservation; about developing intuitive boundaries; and about natural consequences and the importance of collaboration and mutual protection.

To lose these connections—my relationships with the growers, bakers, shoppers, market vendors and the community my family found there—would be a real shame, I reminded myself many times as I tallied my economic losses.

It was that feeling that comes from sharing a passion for something that hooked me right from the start, and that is precisely what kept me going all those years, kept me in the game long after I should have called it a day.

And believe me, I had plenty of chances to call it a day, especially after the major setbacks that I experienced. After the bear attacked the grain shed, for example, I could have called it quits. Who else would keep milling in a shed at the edge of a vast expanse of wilderness populated by wheat-loving bears? But somehow I kept going. And after the van's transmission broke, I could have bowed out without a hint of "I told you so" from my friends. Who else would keep using a vehicle that couldn't back up?

At least if I had put in my chips and cashed out, I could have blamed the outcome on outside forces, external circumstances beyond my control. But because I had risen to those challenges and triumphed over adversity, it gave me hope. I overcame those challenges by doing what I've always done in a tough situation: I put my head down and tried harder.

It was not easy to stay motivated as my costs rose and my sales declined, but I forged ahead. I could see the writing on the wall, but I didn't want to read what was written, because I already knew what it said. And I wasn't willing to—or wasn't able to, more accurately—give up, because that would mean giving up the relationships I'd built over the years.

For most businesses, the end user is the consumer. And in many cases, that was how the Flour Peddler worked, too: the farmers' market shopper took home my value-added product and baked a loaf of bread. But the final destination of this multi-faceted enterprise wasn't always a farmers' market customer, because I was also doing education and outreach, which provided a new avenue for relationships.

I think back to the excited faces of the kids in the gymnasium as we ground flour and rode the bike mill. I did a total of eight school presentations, and each time it was unique and exciting. I had thought these elementary school presentations would be the extent of my educational outreach, but then I got the chance to try something truly unique.

In March 2011, I designed a project specifically for the urban environment that would encourage home owners to convert their front lawns into micro-fields of wheat by showing them some of the absurdities and contradictions inherent in industrial-scale agriculture. The idea began with a set amount of space: one hundred square feet of grass would be dug up and amended as necessary, and grain seeds would be scattered. Then, if all went well, it would grow tall and strong. When it was ripe, gardeners from the local community would work together to harvest the wheat and bring it to a central location, where we would thresh it and mill it with Flour Peddler bike-mill technology. The end goal: a feast involving this "hyper local" Vancouver wheat.

For adamant foodies, the notion of "hyper local" was connected to the larger assumption that local meant better (in a holistic sense of the word better) and therefore the more local, the better. If provincial procurement was good, one hundred miles was better, and ten miles—or one mile—was nearing local-food purity.

Of course, the question of whether closer is always better is one open for debate. Many local food activists fall victim to "the local trap," a term coined by Brandon Born and Mark Purcell to describe the "tendency of food activists and researchers to assume something inherent about the local scale." It makes the local scale *imply* a socially enacted and more environmentally just food system. While there is some evidence that, in the case of the grain chain, this local scale leads to more personal relationships, we can't assume this is always the case with local food. The products that the Flour Peddler offered and, in fact, the entire manifesto were built around the slippery edge of the local trap. But while the trap is set in many local food interactions, being reflexive is key. And in terms of educating urban consumers, five-mile wheat growing on boulevards and in schoolyards happened to be the most suitable tool.

The Environmental Youth Alliance (EYA) saw an opportunity. They had been looking to expand the scope of the school education about food systems and seed sovereignty, so they agreed to provide administrative support and organize a pilot project in the spring/summer of 2011. The EYA applied to the City of Vancouver for a five-thousand-dollar grant, which would fund the coordination efforts and administration of the Lawns to Loaves outreach work in a number of public schools throughout Vancouver. The grant application was successful, and on May 1, 2011, a few dozen of us gathered at the Strathcona Community Gardens in East Vancouver to discuss the plan and practise spreading seeds. After we seeded the test plot, we each took envelopes full of red spring wheat seeds to plant in our own spaces.

The goal of this project, Lawns to Loaves, was never about growing wheat in the city. Contrary to popular belief, it was not a food security project, nor was it an attempt to increase capacity for urban food production. Instead, Lawns to Loaves was an educational experiment, helping people understand the dynamics involved in grain production by shrinking the scale to ridiculous levels: wheat grown in plots of one hundred square feet, hand threshed, milled by bicycle. We would be questioning and challenging the dominant model—the idea that there's only one way to grow (gigantic Prairie farms) and process (industrial-scale mills) grains.

The restrictive space proved to be the most interesting part of the project. Some people only had a planter box on their apartment deck. Other people used potting containers. Josh and I dug up a section of his front boulevard and sowed seeds. One avid urban farmer and writer stretched the conceptual and actual boundaries of the micro-field concept beyond my expectations. Vancouver resident (and master gardener) Andrea Bellamy organized a group of volunteers who prepped, seeded and harvested a plot of eight hundred square feet just off Victoria Drive and East 21st Avenue. Cars rushed by and the SkyTrain hummed overhead as the golden wheat waved in the breeze. This wheat field produced 75 percent of the first year's harvest.

In late spring, the Lawns to Loaves project finally got noticed by the media, but not in the way we had anticipated.

It turned out that some Vancouver city councillors were less than thrilled about using taxpayer dollars to fund what Councillor Suzanne Anton referred to as a "goofy" project, especially when there were "real issues" on the table (like the policing costs associated with the 2011 Stanley Cup riots and the non-violent Occupy Vancouver protest). Combined with the media criticism of the new separated bike lanes, and the bylaw allowing the keeping of chickens, the stage was set for a political showdown.

For a three-week period, versions of the Lawns to Loaves story ran in the *West Ender*, the *Georgia Straight, Metro/24 Hours, Burnaby Now* and the *Vancouver Sun*, and on CBC. Unfortunately, most of this media attention failed to grasp the broader goals of the project. Of the five thousand dollars of grant money, not a single cent was given to growers or harvesters. Instead, it funded 100 percent of the EYA initiatives in schools across Vancouver (involving over 230 students in total) and paid a small stipend to EYA administrators and organizers for their work in mapping, communicating with and supporting the thirty-five growers. There was some ridicule about the sixty kilograms of wheat we hoped to produce, using the five-thousand-dollar grant amount and dividing by the number of kilograms, producing an outrageous cost-per-unit analysis.

After a month, the media storm died down, but the wheat kept growing.

So it was with mixed emotions that we harvested all the wheat on a warm August evening. Threshing it by hand took half a day, then we milled it using the Flour Peddler bikes, prepared and kneaded pizza dough and feasted on "hyper local" pizza. Whatever happened next, we had actually grown wheat in the city and seen it through, ending up with the tastiest, and certainly the most local, whole-wheat pizza crust around.

The wheat brought a group together; we laboured and laughed alongside one another. And the legacy of the Lawns to Loaves project was the understanding it gave Vancouver schoolchildren of the role wheat plays in building community, not to mention the chance to see it grow in their own neighbourhood.

When I look back on it now, I see why it was so hard to let go.

It wasn't only that I wanted the relationships, needed them, even. It was also that I felt responsible for those relationships. I had created them, after all, and without me, I was certain they would fall apart. If I gave up and packed it in, I told myself, I would be severing the links that bound grain farmers, producers and consumers across the southern part of this province. This responsibility hung like a weight on my shoulders.

By spring 2012, the business was in a tailspin. Everyone was suffering "f%*king Flour Peddler" burnout (as Amanda-Rae and I called it whenever the kids weren't around), and another season was looming.

I evaluated the toll it was taking on everyone, most notably my family.

Amanda-Rae, who had been a tireless advocate of the Flour Peddler for the first few years, had well and truly moved on. At the beginning, she staffed farmers' market booths for me, stood on the front lines at agricultural fairs, milled and bagged at least half a tonne of flour, talked to overly excited or irate customers on the phone, cleaned the grain shed after a powerhouse day of milling (while I drank a beer) and even tried to keep some records.

From the early daydreams of grandeur, through the high times, to the days of the broken market tents, broken van transmission and a whole vanload of broken promises—"I'll shut it down after this season, I promise you!"—Amanda-Rae had, just like Tammy Wynette, stood by her man.

But one day, the markets had lost their appeal for Amanda-Rae. She passed the phone over the moment someone said they were looking for flour. She drank beer while I milled seventy-five kilograms and cleaned up. She didn't even want to know about the finances anymore. As far as she was concerned, that ship had sailed.

Even Mom and Dad's support was waning. But they never lost hope. Well, actually they did, on multiple occasions, saying things like, "I hope this market will be better than the last dozen," or "Chris, this is hopeless. You might consider shutting it down," or "We've lost all hope in this." But what they never withdrew from me was their love, support, compassion and coffee. They supported me while I supported my failing business, the drive to help their child in times of need overpowering their rational thought.

In late spring 2012, I got a call from Hannah Wittman, my academic supervisor. She told me I had been accepted to the PhD program in the Faculty of Land and Food Systems at UBC. Suddenly, I had a more-than-legitimate reason to get out. But I was plagued by anxiety. How could I let these connections fall apart? Was my food activism not strong enough to sustain it?

I decided there was an option between staying put and getting out: sell the Flour Peddler business. That way, I told myself, I could be assured that those links, which I'd worked so hard to build, would continue and grow.

The succession plan was ingenious, as far as I was concerned: sell an electric production mill, a bike mill, a table, several Rubbermaid basins and a large wooden sign as a package to any budding entrepreneur in Canada or abroad. What city in North America couldn't benefit from an economically inefficient, labour-intensive, educational freak show like the Flour Peddler at their farmers' market? Of course, each owner/operator would be responsible for sourcing their own grain from their own farmers and building relationships with marketing and distribution points throughout their specific area.

There were very few takers. Maybe I was asking too much, or maybe I just wasn't able to get the word out to a wide enough audience. Or maybe—just maybe—I sabotaged it, because I couldn't bear to part with it. I mean, who else could be the Flour Peddler?

Part of the Flour Peddler was the persona—the in-depth knowledge of grain systems that I had developed through years of sociological research and observation. The Flour Peddler was a character of mythological proportions, always ready with baking advice or a wisecrack, possessing the charisma that could charm the wheat from the chaff. The next Flour Peddler would be at a disadvantage, I told myself, although, admittedly, probably a better business operator.

In the end, I talked myself out of letting go for so long that by the time I was forced to let go, there was no succession plan. There was a brand and some committed customers, but there was no business—just a jumble of market booth supplies and five years of memories.

Like Gollum in *The Lord of the Rings*, who cannot bear the thought of life without his precious, I was obsessed. And this obsession had been working against my better judgment. I had to do what was right for Middle Earth and say goodbye. The Flour Peddler, I finally admitted, was not a business that could be packaged and sold. Rather, it was a unique, multi-faceted and volatile edifice of my own creation. The Flour Peddler was me—and it couldn't be anyone else, though Josh did an admirable job of covering for me at the Vancouver markets. I worked myself to the bone, trying to be the missing link in southwestern BC's grain chain. The Flour Peddler connected people throughout our province—a tractor-driving grain farmer in Armstrong to an urban condo-dwelling graphic designer in Vancouver's West End—but its underlying philosophy nearly bankrupted me.

And that's right about the time Josh brought up the subject of South Sudan.

He didn't time it this way, but Josh approached me when I was down and out. I had lost all hope in the business and wanted nothing more to do with grains, ever. Every stray kernel in my coat pocket or on the floor of my car was a reminder of the futility of it all. The overdue invoices from Fieldstone Organics Granary kept piling up. The raspy sound of the mill haunted my dreams. I think I even swore off pancakes for a whole week.

"We could direct the Flour Peddler profits towards the trip," he mused. I asked him how he intended to do it.

I had decided this was the last season we would sell at the farmers' markets. It just didn't make sense anymore, transporting a product from the interior of BC by truck to Vancouver, then up to the Sunshine Coast on a ferry, where it would be milled and brought back to Vancouver to sell.

"What about doing once-per-month deliveries?" he persisted. I considered it.

Maybe there was another way to sell the grain, I agreed. I had co-organized that Urban Grains CSA with Jim, FarmFolk CityFolk, Ayla and Martin, hadn't I? Maybe we could use that as a template, and just add our own spin?

In the end, Josh and I developed a Community Supported Processor program—a monthly delivery service for our loyal customers. If we could convert some of our one-off customers into monthly subscribers, and turn those subscribers into supporters of our "Business As (Un)usual" campaign, we might be able to raise enough money for a trip to South Sudan.

We decided to give it a shot. In the summer of 2012, we began collecting email addresses from our customers and connecting with them electronically, rather than face-to-face at the farmers' markets. This monthly newsletter advertised our products, spread our message and revolutionized the way we did business.

We weren't the first ones to develop a Community Supported Processor (CSP) program for milled flour. But I can say we took the template and ran with it.

A CSP allows interested community members to purchase shares with a local producer or processor, in our case, a miller. The CSP model shares many similarities with the Community Supported Agriculture (CSA) concept, where customers become shareholders in the output of a farm and receive a weekly box throughout the growing season. In our case, a bag of flour is delivered to a subscriber's front porch. This food-based connection creates a relationship of trust between the shareholder and the miller, and offers mutual benefits: a nutritious and fresh product for the shareholder, and guaranteed work and income for the miller. The CSP model reduces the time and financial investment involved in travelling to and being physically present at each and every farmers' market, and reduces the risk involved in preparing a substantial amount of flour, a product that we believed must be consumed fresh if it is to be valued.

Though it bypasses the farmers' market completely, the CSP relies on a vendor presence at a market or other venue to initiate the relationship. In other words, it only worked for us because we had already spent four years at the Trout Lake and Kitsilano markets, building relationships with customers based on trust, traceability, authenticity and personality. While a farmers' market customer can choose to purchase or not on a given week, depending on many variables (available time, available money, level of interest, number of bags they are carrying already), the CSP customer has already made a commitment. We turned some one-time purchasers into consistent farmers' market customers, and some long-time farmers' market shoppers into dedicated CSP subscribers.

And it was the purchases by those CSP subscribers that got us to South Sudan.

10

Aweil

We're in Aweil, but the bike mill isn't. Yet. William thinks the *matatu* transporting it must be past Rumbek by now. It left Juba Saturday morning, when William paid the driver to strap it to the roof.

We landed in Aweil on Sunday, and woke Monday morning to news of the attempted coup and reports of hundreds of people killed. The situation inside the country was critical, the news reported. Dad was texting Josh every few hours, checking on us and trying to relay what he thought might be useful information. We knew that the Juba airport was closed and a curfew had been imposed. We decided that all we could do was keep Dad updated. We were scheduled to fly back to Juba on Thursday, after we completed the bike-mill workshop in Panlang, a three-hour drive away.

Now, all we need is for the bike mill to arrive.

To take our minds off the matter at hand, Josh and I wander among the shelters inside the UN's World Food Programme compound, where we are staying. Our rooms are in a squat cinderblock building with concrete floors, thin mattresses and torn mosquito nets. The squat toilet and cold-water shower are across the yard in another cement block.

It feels like we're camping. We're the lucky ones; we could be camping for real. Throughout the yard, there are several old canvas tents where other development workers without deep pockets are housed.

There is a veranda in the centre of the yard, where the caterer will serve breakfast, William assured us. But when we woke at 8:00 a.m. this morning, we saw no signs of activity. We continue wandering, following footpaths through the clusters of nearby huts. You really get a sense of the scale of this country on the fringes of Aweil. In Juba, there are buildings and infrastructure, and the hustle and bustle of urban life, so it feels like any number of populous African cities. But out here in Aweil, temporary homes of woven-grass huts replace concrete high-rises, and people migrate with their animals.

In Juba, the obvious reference point is the country's southern neighbour, Uganda. But in Aweil, this close to the northern border, you can feel Sudan calling. This area is the overlap zone between more settled farmers and semi-nomadic herders. While these populations have coexisted for centuries, if not thousands of years, the past half-century brought increased conflict to the region as various groups took to arming themselves, either for defensive or offensive means. The border is a stark reminder of how relations between the mainly Arab Muslims and the Black African Christians broke down due to repressive governmental policies, resulting in massive population displacement, starvation and a series of civil wars that culminated in the country being split in two, between north and south.

Before this division in 2011, the country of Sudan was one of Africa's largest: nearly 2.5 million square kilometres. For centuries, the region had been influenced (but not controlled) by Arab slave traders along the Nile River. In the early 1800s, as Ottoman rule in Egypt solidified, a keen interest developed in the southern region, especially around the Sudd, the vast swamps of the Nile. After Pasha Muhammad Ali made incursions, the British bombed Alexandria and subsequently invaded Egypt in 1882. The area south of Egypt became known as Anglo-Egyptian Sudan. After a Mahdi revolt led to the brief fall of Khartoum, Lord Kitchener fought the famous

Battle of Omdurman (near Khartoum) in 1898, which solidified British control. The British now administered a huge swathe of territory south from the Egyptian border all the way to the Belgian Congo and the upper reaches of Uganda and Lake Victoria.

The British categorized and administered Sudan as a binary: the Muslim North and the Christian South; the Arab African and the Black African. By the 1950s, when it became clear that independence was approaching, agitation grew, especially in the south, many arguing that "Black Christians" would not consent to being ruled by "Arab Muslims." But in 1956, the newly independent country of Sudan was born—a single country with guaranteed equal rights for all.

In the decades following Sudan's independence, southerners claimed marginalization, forced Islamization and attacks by government forces against civilians. Armed groups emerged and loosely coalesced into the Sudan People's Liberation Army (SPLA), officially established on May 16, 1983. John Garang emerged as leader and led the SPLA until 1991, when Riek Machar and Lam Akol tried to overthrow him, sparking infighting and the creation of an SPLA–Nasir faction representing Machar's territory. Infighting led to reprisal killings across the south, notably the killing of two thousand civilians in Bor in 1991. However, the groups co-operated sufficiently until the ceasefire in 2005, which led to the Comprehensive Peace Agreement and eventually the referendum on independence. After fifty-five years of being ruled by Khartoum, the people of South Sudan received their own country.

The road through Aweil town is paved, which surprises me. "When the civil war was ending and the Comprehensive Peace Agreement was signed in 2005, it allowed for a referendum to be held in the south, whether to stay in Sudan or form our own country." We're sitting inside the cab of the truck now, and William talks over his shoulder to us. "It was after the CPA that the Khartoum government started coming to our municipalities, offering to build infrastructure, to invest money. It was clearly a buy-off, and people were angry. Most refused the money, saying that Khartoum had been bombing and killing them for decades and that they would not accept anything from the North.

"But our governor said yes to the investment from Khartoum, and in Aweil town they built this paved road. At first, people were mad, because they saw it as a betrayal of the cause, but the governor was not worried. Then, when it came time for the vote, the people in Aweil voted in favour of independence. Then the governor told the people, 'All those who rejected the money, they have independence. And now we in Aweil also have independence—and pavement!'" William breaks out laughing and thumps the dashboard. "That guy was smart," he says, and then swerves to avoid some kids walking along the road and kicking a tattered soccer ball. "The people here, they think the road is a sidewalk. When it was first paved, there were very few cars in Aweil, so the local people thought it was made for them, so their feet didn't get dusty." He chuckles. "Just look at this one!" he says, steering around a woman carrying a jerry can on her head while walking her children down the middle of the road. She shoots him a dirty look as we pass.

In South Sudan, William explains, many crops are grown seasonally to take advantage of the summer rains. Sow seeds in early spring, wait for the summer deluge and then harvest during the dry season.

"This is the traditional way," William says. "But this way—relying on the rainy season—means we can only produce a single crop in a year."

In William's mind, South Sudan could be a model for food security in the East Africa region. While we look out the window and see arid terrain, he sees possibility. After all, he says, there is plenty of sun and the water table is high. The only thing that is lacking is a way to get the water from underground. "So this was my idea: to create a dry-season alternative for farmers here in Aweil."

After a few minutes, we turn off the paved road and pull up beside a patchwork of fields. William points to the back of the fields, where blocks of verdant green leafy plants are growing.

"This is the Aweil urban farm," he tells us. "I tried to label it on Google Earth when I was back in Canada, but I'm not sure if it worked, and I cannot check it from here." He laughs.

As we get out of the truck and walk along the edges of the tilled fields, I hear the familiar sound of an engine running. I ask William if it is a generator. He shakes his head, smiling. "You are very used to this sound, being in South Sudan," he says. "No, that is the sound of success."

We walk towards the lush greenery at the back of the field, following a gush of water, which flows along the hand-carved channels above the plots. We stop next to a large hole, about ten feet deep and twenty feet across. There's water in the hole, and there's a diesel pump sitting on top with a long hose stretching down to suck up the water, then another hose sending it into the channels and along to the fields. We watch it flow along, being diverted to different fields filled with potatoes. "We are even trying to produce rice here," William says. "Just imagine that!"

William started this farm two years ago as a way to take advantage of the things South Sudan has plenty of: sunshine, a high water table and willing participants. What the farm has done, he tells us, is create hundreds of individual entrepreneurs, all of whom co-operate to keep the water flowing.

"When we started out, there were eight people who were involved," he says. "I told them I was not paying any money—that I didn't want employees; I wanted business partners. I told them that I had the pump, but they had to dig the hole to access the water and then till the fields to ready them for planting. That way, everyone who was involved had a stake in the outcome. I told them that at first, I would pay for the diesel for the water pump. But once they sold their first crops, they would have to contribute to purchase the next jerry can of diesel to keep the pump running."

I nod. It's pretty much a pitch-perfect form of international development, the kind every NGO agency would love to have in their portfolio—where simple technology is introduced, but where local people invest their time and energy to do the work, and they reap the rewards. "But there was one guy, he didn't like this model," William says. "He said he preferred that I pay him. So I said okay, if that's what you want. I told him I would pay one SSP (South Sudan pound) per day, the standard rate for farming labour. He agreed, and started working for me, growing my crops alongside the others. After two months, he harvested my crops, and then I went and sold them at the Aweil market and made five hundred SSP. Then I paid him his sixty SSP for his labour.

"The day after the market, that guy quit working for me and decided to start working for himself. And now," William says, smiling, "that man is the most productive of them all."

It's not the siren call of fresh local produce and foodies that is driving William's urban farm; it's a response to remote locations and bad infrastructure. With the exception of foreign workers living on the UN bases, most of the people of Aweil are eating local food by default. Soon restaurants in town will be using these crops, he assures us, and the people are working with purpose to feed themselves and their communities.

And now, thanks to William's work through the Pan Aweil Development Agency, the people of Aweil can grow crops year-round. It's just one of the initiatives that William has started, with the support of a small group of Canadian philanthropists who looked at South Sudan and saw what William saw: potential.

It would be easy to see the Pan Aweil Development Agency as a one-man show. With a budget of less than forty thousand dollars annually, William implements on-the-ground projects through PADA, as he calls it for short. No commercials with pictures of starving orphans, no vague semantics or romantic visions of eternal happiness. None of the donations are filtered through a labyrinth of bureaucracy. All the money goes to fund local, needs-based development.

But William would be the first to tell you that PADA is not a solo operation. For him, a development agency is inseparable from the people it works with, so while William doesn't have any direct employees, he does have the help and support of the community—something many international NGOs would envy.

William takes out his cellphone and shows us a picture of a tall cement box. "This is a rural area water filtration system, but we just call it a biosand filter. These ones can be built by the people themselves. You fill the concrete box with gravel, small crushed rocks and sand, then you pour the water in the top, and when it comes out at the bottom, the people have clean water."

The process is simple. As the water percolates through the different grades of sediment, waterborne pathogens remain where they are, eaten up by the bio-organisms, resulting in clean water for communities.

"After we installed the first hand-pump in Aweil," he says, "we discovered that it is very expensive. So when I went back to Canada, I found out that an organization in Calgary, the Centre for Affordable Water and Sanitation Technology, had invented this biosand filtration system. CAWST brought me to their office for a training course, and now I am starting to introduce them here in South Sudan. These first ones are in Terekeka, about fifty kilometres from Juba. If they are a success, we will bring them to Aweil and the rural areas."

William prefers the biosand filter, because local people can be trained to build it. The filters retail for the equivalent of sixty US dollars each, but rural people can pay with animals. "Maybe they can trade a cow or a flock of goats for it. That way everyone has to contribute, but everyone is paying in a way they can afford." Even the poorest people, the ones with no animals, can buy one, William explains, if they bring bricks. "We call it 'Brick for Filter.' We tell them they should make three hundred bricks. Then we use the bricks to build a school. That way, they pay for the filter, and the kids get a school."

I smile. William knows context-appropriate development, I think to myself.

"Whenever Pan Aweil is commissioned to build a school," he says, "the first thing I do is visit that place, so I can find out where the children are gathering." NGOs can spend fifty thousand dollars to build a very nice school, William explains, but no kids will come if it is in the wrong place, like in the middle of a field or a clearing, which is where he says some foreign agencies seem to want to build them.

"But build the school next to their tree," he says, "and the kids will come."

The next morning, Josh and I wake up early. There's no movement on the veranda, so we decide to go look for some other breakfast options.

As we walk to the road, the chill of the air still upon us, Josh asks me how I slept. I roll my eyes. "Terrible," I say. "Did you hear me yell in the night?" I fell asleep wearing all my clothes to keep warm, woke in a panic when I found I was tangled in my mosquito netting and then called out for help.

"No," Josh says. "I was tucked up in my sleeping bag, head under everything."

I quietly cursed him for having had the foresight to bring a sleeping bag to a country that recorded some of the hottest temperatures on the planet. William told us that in Aweil, December was the coldest month, just like in Canada. Though daytime temperatures of 35° Celsius meant it was on a different scale from Canada, he was right—it was surprisingly cold at night. In Juba, we had fallen asleep sweltering under fans, with only a brief cool-down period before dawn. But in Aweil, seven hundred kilometres north, there were massive temperature fluctuations. The sun pounded our heads like a jackhammer by day, but once it dropped, the air cooled quickly, and by bedtime we were wearing sweaters.

Josh said it felt like we were nearing the Sahara Desert, the massive expanse of sand that stretches clear across the widest portion of the African continent, from Mauritania in the west to Sudan in the east. Josh has been to both sides of the Sahara, having visited Morocco, Algeria and Tunisia, as well as the ancient trading outpost of Timbuktu in Mali.

As we approach the pavement, we hail down a passing *tuk-tuk*. We get in, but the driver has no idea where to take us. "Aweil town?" Josh suggests. The driver doesn't move, shrugs his shoulders. I point up the road, the way the *tuk-tuk* was already travelling. "Aweil town?" I say again. This time, it registers, and he sets off, the cold wind giving us the shivers as we close the fabric flaps on the sides.

We roll through the centre of town, passing the cluster of roadside shops, but see little activity, just animal herders walking their goats along the road. Then suddenly, I spot a sign: BJ's Restaurant. I point to it. "There!" I say to the driver, who swings over and lurches to a stop. We offer him two South Sudanese pounds, but he shakes his head, shows four fingers. We give him three pounds, and he drives off.

Josh and I balance single file along a wobbly two-by-six board bridging an open drainage ditch. We step inside the restaurant. The interior is dark, but we can see a few people sitting at a long wooden table, plates of greasy *samosas* and steaming mugs of tea in front of them. They turn and stare at us. A woman appears from behind a plywood wall, wiping her hands on her apron. She stops and looks at us like we just arrived from outer space. We say hi, gesture to the table and sit down.

"I get the sense that they don't see too many UN workers or other foreign people in this place," Josh says.

"You'd think they would be used to people seeking them out," I reply, "them being pretty much the only game in town."

Eventually, the woman approaches us, but she waits for us to initiate the order. I point to a cup of tea, and Josh points to a *samosa*, lifting two fingers. She turns to go. Ten minutes pass. I peer behind the curtain into the back, just in time to see a woman using a bucket to slosh water over the floor, washing food waste into the gutter. I hear a goat bleat, and see it's tethered to a stake in the back of the yard.

A tarnished silver plate arrives bearing two *samosas*. The mugs of tea are clunked down beside it. There is no sugar for the tea or napkins for the greasy pastry. Just as we dig in, Josh's phone rings. It's William. He asks Josh where we are, and Josh explains we are at a place called BJ's Restaurant. I listen to Josh explain it again, like William can't understand where we are. The people around us are watching us like we're extras in the wrong movie.

We finish up the *samosas* and tea, pay some money—it was never clear what the actual price was, so we give the woman five pounds and she doesn't ask for more—and exit onto the street. The sun has fully risen now, but there is still not much in the way of shopkeeper activity in Aweil.

I flag down another *tuk-tuk*. He is unclear where we want to go—WFP compound? We try various combinations of letters, but nothing works. Eventually, he speeds along, drops us at the UN compound gates and drives away, having earned three pounds for a two-minute trip.

William calls again. Now we're somewhere along the road, Josh tells him. We took a *tuk-tuk*, he explains, but it dropped us at the UN compound, not the WFP compound where we are staying. We are just walking back now, we say.

When we arrive at the WFP gate, William is there, smiling. "You guys," he says, laughing. "That BJ's place is the same one that caters the breakfast here." He points towards the shelter, where a teenaged girl is serving up greasy *samosas* and steaming mugs of tea.

"You guys are hilarious!" William says.

Just before 2:00 p.m., William's phone rings. It's the *matatu* driver, he says. The mill has arrived. It took a grand total of fifty-eight hours to travel the seven hundred kilometres from Juba. William leaves us at the WFP compound—"Remember, if they see you, we will have to pay a much higher price!"—and he heads out in his pickup truck, returning forty-five minutes later with the bike mill lying in the back.

We peer over the side of the truck with trepidation. The bike mill has travelled some of the worst roads in the country, with luggage loaded and unloaded on top, around and inside its bright-green frame. Josh and I can only hope that there is no damage, or at least that no crucial part is broken.

Our eyes scan the bike mill: the sprocket, the chain, the handlebars. It's all there, all still welded together. The only damage we can find is one broken footpad from the pedal on the right side. We exhale with relief.

"Yes," William says. "It is actually a good thing that the pedal is broken. The driver wanted to charge me more money than what we agreed upon back in Juba, but I was able to point to this damage and ask for a discount. So we settled on the original price of three hundred pounds—about seventy-five US dollars."

We need to get a new set of pedals, we tell William. In fact, we should buy an extra bicycle chain as well. And maybe a size twelve metric wrench. "I can get those things at the market," he says, and starts towards the truck, but we stop him.

"We want to go this time," I say. "Even if the price is a bit higher, we still want the experience of browsing the Aweil market." William shrugs, and we climb in.

We wade into the Aweil market, clearly not one of Lonely Planet's top choices. There are no handicrafts, no artisan products, but plenty of truck tires, sheet metal, bags of concrete and bike pedals. We buy several sets. I also decide we need some yellow paint to print the name of the bike mill on the side. The man at the shop sells us the paint, but he won't let us buy it without also buying paint thinner. We fork over the cash, even though we aren't sure we even need the thinner.

Josh and I spend the afternoon preparing the bike mill for its final journey. I paint PADA (for Pan Aweil Development Agency) in bright yellow letters on the side and add accent colours beneath the handlebars (without the use of paint thinner). Then I stand back, and Josh snaps photos.

"It is pretty rugged, hey bro?" Josh calls out from behind the lens of his camera.

"The best one ever," I say.

"How about the best one *yet*?" he answers.

That night, William takes us to the main UN compound for dinner and drinks. We are signed in by the guards, the large blue doors opening just as they had upon our arrival after the helicopter trip two days earlier. We walk towards a thatched-roof hut that is decorated with world flags and boasts a flat-screen television, mounted in the rafters. This is the *tukul*, William explains, a structure modelled after a South Sudanese shelter.

We reflexively order a round of beer—Tusker for Josh and William, Bell for me—but then I realize I'm standing in front of the best-stocked bar I've seen since the Kampala hostel, so I cancel my order and choose from one of the several kinds of rum on offer. The server cracks a Coke and pours it over the rum on ice. After so many rounds of Bell beer, the first sip of this highball tastes like heaven.

We see the familiar faces of the politicians we met at the Aweil Grand Hotel a few days earlier. We chat for hours about the political situation, about the surprising revelations. No one is sure what is happening, but everyone is sure there is more to the story than is being told.

After three rounds we get up to go, but a gregarious UN worker wants to order another round for everyone. Josh says yes, but I wave her off, saying I'm finished. "I don't care if you're Finnish," she says. "You can drink with me!" Another rum and Coke appears. I shake my head and laugh, knowing that I can't avoid another drink.

William explains that there is a gate at the back of the UN compound, the same one we followed that first day when we arrived, and if Josh and I go through that gate and cross the soccer field, we will up end inside the back of our accommodation inside the WFP compound. We stumble back under the glow of the moonlight. At the gate, two young men wearing baggy military uniforms and brandishing guns check our names against the list. "Herga?" one asks, pointing at me. "Heema?" pointing at Josh. We shrug, and find our names on their list so we don't have to spell it out.

As we approach the doors of our rooms, we hear the sounds of drumming and chanting. Josh and I look at each other. He grabs his voice recorder, and we head out, following the pulsating beats to a churchyard, where we find a procession taking place. The kid at the front is holding a large wooden cross, and the people are dancing along behind it, the drummers pounding out a driving rhythm.

Josh holds out his voice recorder, and we both start shaking to the music. The priest approaches us and asks where we are from. Canada, we say. "It is a cold place, just like Aweil at night," he says. "Come, dance with us. You will stay warm."

We dance for more than half an hour, following the procession as it winds in a figure eight pattern in the dirt courtyard under the light of the moon. When we finally break from the group to head back, they wish us luck on the next phase of our journey, and make us promise to come back one day.

11

The Road to Panlang

"Until six years ago, there was no road to Marial Bai."

We dip and dive through potholes the size of bomb craters. William pilots the truck along the dirt road, then drives off the side and down a steep hill to a sandy track, which we follow until it too gives out, forcing us to head back up to the roadbed. We cross a mess of potholes, then drop down the other side to not so much a road as a trail carved through thorny bushes. In some sense, there still is no road to Marial Bai.

"In the rainy season I will not be able to get here," William says. "Or I will go, but it will take all day." I admire his effort, especially given how much time transport eats up and how rough it is on the vehicle.

We pass people walking along the road, balancing firewood or lugging jerry cans. I realize how easy we have it here in this truck. There is no air conditioning in the cab; we are already sticky with sweat, and we can't roll the windows down because of the dust that hangs in the air, but I can't imagine having to walk along this road with the sun beating down.

As we bump along the road, dust-covered children in torn clothes throw handfuls of dirt into the gigantic potholes. "These kids do this to show the drivers that they are trying to fix the road," William says. "Then they hope the drivers will throw some small amount of money out the window, leaving them to fight over coins in the dust." It's a tragic but apt illustration of the half-century of underinvestment, neglect and active destruction of southern infrastructure by the northern government in Khartoum.

"I never throw money out the window to these kids," William says. "I think it's not a good idea. The more people give them money, even if the intentions are noble, the more the children become accustomed to doing it. Instead of doing something productive, they become like beggars."

The radio crackles as William searches for a signal. "There must be some news about the situation," he says. That's what he's been calling it for the last two days—"the situation"—the violence that is now spreading through the northern and central regions of his country.

Over the past two days, the message from President Salva Kiir Mayardit and the official South Sudanese media has been consistent: armed men loyal to Vice-President Riek Machar tried to stage a coup after political talks failed to reach a consensus. Of course, given that the only domestic media accredited to operate are those that toe the official line, there is no way to independently verify this information. The only truly independent news outlets, *Sudan Tribune* and Radio Tamazuj, are based in Europe, so they have to rely on local knowledge, which means they can't verify anything either.

Riek Machar has "disappeared," the media reports, implying that a wanted man leaving town is tantamount to an admission of guilt. There is a short clip stating that Machar has denied all allegations of staging the coup, but they note that Machar stands behind his earlier remarks that President Kiir is a dictator and no longer fit to lead the country. The report ends with speculation about where Machar is hiding, likely near the city of Bor in Jonglei State, one hundred kilometres north of the capital, Juba.

To observers of South Sudanese politics, this conclusion

would not be surprising. While Jonglei State may be located inside the country of South Sudan in geographic terms, it has never really been under the control of the central government—what political analysts refer to as the difference between *de jure* and *de facto* control: in theory and in reality. For decades, Jonglei State has been home to various rebel groups, from small collectives of ragtag bandits, to the powerful private army headed by David Yau Yau. Even after South Sudan achieved its independence from Khartoum in 2011, some rebel groups have actively opposed the official government in Juba, while others have entered into fragile peace treaties and ad hoc ceasefire agreements. So it's not a stretch to see how Jonglei State might play host to fighters harbouring anti-government sentiment now, although at the moment, no one can be sure of precisely what is happening.

"The places where Dinka and Nuer tribes overlap will be the hardest hit," William says. "Because the president is a Dinka and the vice-president is a Nuer, it is only too easy to make it about tribes. It was not about tribes. It was about politics. But now, people with bad intentions will use this as an excuse."

William can see the writing on the wall. What began as a political dispute between a president and his vice-president is now morphing into a full-blown conflict along ethnic lines. In hindsight, it was predictable: when the representatives of the two most powerful tribes in South Sudan position themselves on opposite sides of the political divide, it's all too easy for the violence to take on tribal overtones. And in a newly formed country like South Sudan, borders alone cannot bind its citizens together.

Whatever the theories behind it, the outcome is fear and mistrust of the other side, and a lack of faith in the government's ability to ensure safety. The media reports that tens of thousands of civilians have fled their homes, flocking to UN bases around the country, which have opened their doors to the masses. On the radio, UN representative Joe Contreras says the UN is doing its best to cope with the already overwhelming influx of civilians, but that the situation is critical. A rapidly unfolding humanitarian disaster, Contreras calls it—and he warns that if nothing is done to halt the violence, things will get a lot worse.

William clicks off the radio. "I can't listen to this anymore," he says.

As we drive along the road, we pass little huts on stilts, which stand next to the larger family huts. "That is where the family keeps their crops," William says. No corrugated metal walls hold the grain safely inside; kernels slip through cracks and fall below.

World Food Programme figures from May 2014 suggest that around 3.5 million people are facing crisis (2.4 million) or emergency (1.1 million) conditions. This means that nearly 40 percent of the total population is in need of urgent action to ensure adequate nutrition, protect their livelihoods, save lives and prevent famine.

But even before conflict disrupted the food system to this extent, agricultural systems were precarious. From harvesting to drying to threshing and shelling, to winnowing and various stages of transport, grain is lost. Beyond the immediate threat to household food security, post-harvest losses adversely affect farmers and consumers in the lowest income and most vulnerable groups. Post-harvest food losses are a waste of valuable farming inputs, such as water, energy, land, labour and capital. Development agencies, academics and foreign workers agree that investment in post-harvest infrastructure is one of the keys to reducing losses. Most small-scale farmers in sub-Saharan Africa rely on inadequate processing, storage and transportation infrastructure, forcing them to absorb losses, which would represent millions of US dollars.

According to the Africa Postharvest Losses Information System (APHLIS), which provides data on harvest losses, three South Sudanese provinces lost between eight thousand and twenty thousand tonnes of maize in 2004–2007. This weight represents an estimated loss of between 15 and 19 percent, which is a significant portion of a family or community's harvest. Socio-political and environmental impacts are key contributors to overall food insecurity, while rainfall patterns, seasonal flooding, and seed access, as well as pests, diseases and weeds, can spell natural disasters for cereal grain crops, primarily sorghum, maize and smaller local millet varieties. However, the biggest driver of food insecurity on the African continent is conflict.

There are many instances of conflict-generated hunger and deliberately manufactured famines intended to starve out rebellious groups. The Ethiopian experience in 1985—the one that inspired the musical fundraising project Band Aid—was perhaps the most high profile famine, but it was not the only one. Sudan's southern region faced a deliberate campaign of destruction of food growing capacity throughout the civil wars that plagued the country. But now, the perpetrators of South Sudan's conflict are starving their own people.

As William navigates around and through the potholes, I look out at the landscape, a tangle of huts, thorny plants and arid brown earth. But all I can think about right now is whether it's raining in Roberts Creek.

It's mid-December, so the rain at home will be cold, but not yet frigid. Down at the beach, with the blowing wind, the rain pelts your skin and flicks at your face. In the refuge of the thick trees, however, the rain feels gentle, filtering through branches, falling on ferns that gently bend as beads of water appear on them. The flora and fauna suck it up, drink it down, even though it just keeps coming and coming, sometimes for days on end.

The kids will still want to go outside, I think to myself. Amanda-Rae will enforce the requisite raincoats, but they'll be impatient, shoving heels into boots, not wearing socks, even though Mom says they should. Then the slop-squeak sound of rubber on skin will be heard as their little feet tromp off to the squishy trails.

In Vancouver, rain is inconvenient. You step in a puddle on Pender Street before your business meeting, your soaked shoe squeaking down the hallway. Or someone nearly pokes your eye with the tip of an umbrella while shaking it off outside Pacific Centre.

But in the evergreen forest of the Sunshine Coast, the rain is simply part of everyday life, and it is—literally—life-giving. I imagine Solomon chasing Gretchen down the footpath that leads to the pond. I hear them laughing and running down the path strewn with pine needles, nature's offering from the winds of the fall, the winter moss glistening.

We hit a particularly large pothole, and the truck dives down, nearly throwing me out of my seat. I shake my head and grab hold of the dashboard.

The clock on the dash reads 12:30 p.m. William turns on the radio and scans the channels. It's the same recording that was broadcast half an hour earlier, but we listen anyway. The fighting is intense in Malakal, in the northeast of the country, along with Bentiu. Several cities and towns in the northern parts of the country are now considered rebel-held territory. There are reports of people being shot in the streets, roving gangs of young men engaging in tit-for-tat killings. So far, however, Northern Bahr el Ghazal State is peaceful.

William turns off the radio, then bangs the steering wheel. "This makes me mad!" he says. It's the first time I've ever seen

William upset. "These guys should work out their political differences instead of provoking this conflict. Think of how much has been done to attract foreign investment to our country," he continues. "The Lost Boys, we have connections to business people in America and Canada. Some of us even have our own businesses back there. We have brought home all this expertise, all these connections; we have built up the confidence of investors. Think of how much time and effort has been spent negotiating agreements, drafting contracts. But now," he says, his voice dropping, "who will want to invest in South Sudan?"

The question hangs in the air.

"We've spent too long fighting—fighting Khartoum, and now fighting each other. If we have peace, we have stability. If we have stability, we will get investment. And with that investment, we can build up our country.

"But if we don't have peace," William says, "then, well...then we have nothing."

Two-and-a-half hours after leaving Aweil, we arrive at Marial Bai, a roadside collection of one-storey cinderblock buildings. William pulls up next to a shop "to buy soft drinks for the ladies who are coming to your workshop," he explains.

I take the opportunity to get out of the truck and stretch my legs, wandering past shops with bottles of Pepsi displayed in the midday sun. Josh gets out but stays beside the truck. The local boys move closer. I return a few minutes later to find a dozen kids crowded around the truck, peering over at the curious-looking pedal-powered machine.

William appears from the shop carrying a cardboard flat packed with soft drinks. They are not cold, William tell us as he climbs in, so we may not like the taste, but these people have never known otherwise, so however we serve it, it is a treat for them.

"Now," William says as he turns onto a set of tire ruts that lead into the bushes, "let's go to Panlang."

12

The Workshop

I take a sip of warm Pepsi, then begin. "My name is Chris, and this is my brother, Josh. We are from Canada, and we're here today thanks to our good friend, William Kolong. First, we want to say thank you for inviting us here, for welcoming us to Panlang."

I look over at William, and he turns to the crowd gathered under the tree and starts speaking in Dinka. I hear my name, Josh's name and William's last name, and then a few more sentences. And then a few more. Even though I don't understand the words, I enjoy listening to the pace of the language and the rhythm of his speech.

After saying a few more things, William turns back to me. "I cannot just say to them, 'Here are these guys from Canada,' and then you talk more. I have to explain to them who your father is, what is his connection to me, who is your wife's father, the family connection, and so on. And of course, if you had cows, I would tell them how many." He laughs, then continues. "In our place, you need to know the family, the network, how they fit."

I smile and assure him it is no problem. Then I turn back to the crowd.

"Years ago, when William lived in Canada, we talked about this bicycle machine that I had built. I used it to grind grains, which are an important food in Canada. William thought this bike mill would be a good idea for you here, and we thought so too. So today we brought one to Panlang to see if you can use it."

I look over at William and signal that he can translate now. About twenty women, clad in their finest outfits, sit on blue plastic chairs in a semicircle in front of us, their brightly coloured dresses standing out against the brown earth. I watch their faces as William translates, and they nod in understanding. As he talks, he gestures to the bike mill, making a pedalling motion with his hands.

A woman shouts something. William listens, then turns to me. "She is saying that some ladies are worried that, because they do not know how to ride a bicycle, they will fall off. I am telling her that this one is stable, that she cannot fall over."

I put my hands out like I am steadying myself and say, "This is not an actual bicycle; it just has the pedals. So you cannot tip over."

A little more than a year ago, we stood in the Vertex One boardroom, with its black chairs, sparkling or still water and plush carpet, and pitched an idea to John Thiessen to travel to the other side of the planet and build a bike mill. Today, we're delivering that bike mill to the Majok Adim Women's Cooperative.

I reflect on the uniqueness of this situation. I'm presenting to a cluster of people, gathered here, under the village tree. I've given many presentations about local food over the years—about local grain, local farmers, local consumers and local producers. Although the context couldn't be more different, the content is similar, focusing on the importance of local food. But for these people, the choice to eat local isn't really a choice; it's their only option.

"It's important to have control over your food—how it is grown, processed and eaten," I tell them. "This machine doesn't change that, but we think it might help make this process faster and easier."

I ask William if someone can bring some grains so I can demonstrate. He says something in Dinka and a small woman wearing a sparkling white dress darts towards her hut, returning with a tin bowl of golden sorghum. I scoop a handful into the mill, turn the crank, and coarse flour the consistency of cornmeal flows out onto the table. The women quickly brush the flour from the table into a bag, careful not to waste any. In school workshops in Vancouver, I used to have a whole bowl of flour for kids to touch and feel, to play with and then dispose of. Here, one hundred grams blown away was not an acceptable loss.

We put the rest of the sorghum into the mill, and the women stand up from the plastic chairs and move in closer. I pedal the bike mill and watch their eyes light up. The mill cracks the sorghum easily, and it flows out and into the bag. I speed up, the crowd gets bigger, and their voices rise.

They rub it between their fingers, discuss amongst themselves, and then unanimously agree that the grind isn't fine enough. I'm crestfallen. Within seconds, however, they are already proposing ways to sieve it, run it through again or pound it down from this cracked stage.

William says something to the woman, and she and another woman head off. "I am asking her to get her traditional style, the bowl and the stick they use for pounding," William tells me. "Then you can see how much work the ladies do around here."

The women return carrying a long wooden pole and a deep bowl that has been carved from a tree stump. They pour a few handfuls of sorghum in the bowl, then raise the pole up and pound down, using both hands. Thud, thud, thud—the rhythm of rural life.

I tell William I want to try this method. He smiles, but it is a forced smile. "In this place, men do not do this kind of work," he explains. "They will not approve."

I insist, and he explains my request. They squeal and shake their heads. Then, reluctantly, they hand over the pole, hiding their giggles behind their hands.

"You will probably be the first man to touch this pole," William says. "The first white man for sure!"

I lift the pole up, keeping my eye on the bowl below. I don't want to miss and make a fool of myself, nor do I want to hit the edge and break the pole. My first downstrokes are cautious, but after a few solid thuds, I feel I have the rhythm. After a dozen or so, however, I start getting tired.

"We didn't bring this machine here because we think this traditional way of milling is bad," I say, as I stop for breath. "This machine is not meant to be better or worse, just different. You can still do the pounding, but maybe you can use this machine too." I make sure William emphasizes this point. There is a general consensus that yes, this machine is faster.

The small woman in the white dress is the first to try it out. Her feet stretch for the pedals and she chastises William, telling him we should have built this bike mill lower. I signal to her that I want to trade places, and I climb on and stand up on the pedals, showing her how to stand up off the seat. I get off and she climbs on, gingerly positions herself, laughing. Then she starts pedalling, her long dress moving with her. The other women hold the empty corn bag as it fills with flour. After a few minutes, she lets another woman have a turn. Soon, the entire pot of sorghum is milled into a coarse flour.

Doing "development" work is always contentious—and doing development in rural Africa is especially so. Academic and activist Dambisa Moyo calls it a "dead aid" paradigm, in which the cycles of poverty and dependence are reproduced. Others suggest that short-term volunteer and charity projects, though implemented with good intentions, can do more harm than good. The reality is that many people have become sceptical about aid. They rightfully question the degree to which aid can act as a driver and facilitator of progress, and they suggest that in some cases, aid can distort and undermine local institutions and local knowledge, thus acting as a potential obstacle to legitimate progress.

In the months before our departure, numerous colleagues and friends asked me questions about what we felt the impacts of our new technology would be. Would we undermine local market vendors? Would we upset traditional family and gender roles, creating envy or jealousy? Who were we to tell people how they should advance or progress?

They would recite stories about villagers assembling water pipes, then digging them up and selling them once the NGO has pulled out. One of my friends, in a moment of honesty, told me he was fully convinced that the new owners of the bike mill would "sell it for scrap metal as soon as you leave."

As a sociologist, I would say these are all things that we had considered. Frankly, even we had nagging questions. How do we give to others without creating the ego of a beneficent patriarch? How do we equalize the power dynamics that come with variations in access to technology and knowledge? How do we best deliver our idea into a politically and environmentally volatile region?

But upon further reflection, do such questions mean that we shouldn't invest energy in a project? Or does it mean we need to constantly reflect about the range of variables that impact both parties? If the latter is our choice and our intention, is that enough?

Bringing the bike mill here was William's idea, after all. William thought it would make a difference and be appreciated, and because of his track record, we trusted him. Josh and I had no expectations that this bike mill would revolutionize grain milling in South Sudan, only that it might free up some time for women who labour in family food production and processing.

Fundamentally, we did it because William invited us to try. We had made a commitment to him, many years ago in that Metropolis food court, promising to bring a mill to South Sudan and hire local people to build something that could stand up to the rigours of rural life.

And here we are today, following through on that commitment.

In some ways, the Flour Peddler bike-mill project appears about as far from traditional development work as it is possible to get. Rather than funding large infrastructure projects, we were spending money in the local economy. We bought the bus tickets, paid the taxi driver, the engineers, the welders, the *matatu* drivers...and bought the soft drinks. But when you look at it this way, that's exactly what a good development project should do: build local capacity and draw on local knowledge and resources.

In all, Josh and I spent nearly three thousand US dollars in the ground-level South Sudanese economy. In the end, the Majok Adim Women's Cooperative got a bike mill for free, no strings attached. And for our part, we used a bike mill as a means to support local food, to form relationships and to take us on the ride of our lives.

A woman calls out to William. He goes through a short exchange with her, then turns back to us and says, "She is asking how many bike mills you guys brought."

I look over at Josh, but before our eyes connect, William answers, "I told her you only brought this one, because you were not sure if it could work here. I told her it is hard for people from Canada to know if something will be useful here in Panlang. So now she is saying that yes, all these ladies like it, and that next time you come, you should bring more."

The women start discussing amongst themselves, William providing the running dialogue. "See, these ones here, they want to keep the mill where it is, under the tree, because they say it is the most central location. But this one at the back, she lives farther away, and she says it will be hard to bring all her sorghum here to Panlang. She is suggesting that we can move it around to other places."

Josh and I look at each other. We had anticipated this might happen. Questions emerge about our introduction of this technology. Could they organize it so everyone gets a turn? Would it be something that separates them or unites them?

"And these ones," William continues, "they are suggesting we should take it up to the road to Marial Bai, so they can grind sorghum to sell."

This is the hook, the economic opportunity we had pitched: micro-capitalism.

"My sister lives here, and she is already thinking about the business side of things," William explains. "Maybe they can sell flour together at the market and save money to build another one of these bike mills."

William checks his watch. "Chris, we'd better get moving." I nod.

Josh and I drag the bike mill out from under the tree into a clearing. I gesture to the ladies to gather around, and I crouch down beside the bike mill. William directs them to form a semi-circle as Josh snaps photos. Then Josh hands his camera to William and asks him if he can take a shot of both the brothers together. Josh walks towards us, then turns back when he sees William holding the digital camera in his outstretched arm, unsure of how to put his eye on the viewfinder. Josh walks back and changes the settings so the screen shows us in the frame. Then he walks over and positions himself on the other side of the bike mill across from me. We both squint against the hard sun, unsure if William is capturing this moment.

Josh returns to check the settings. Blown-out highlights and black with no detail—a professional photographer's nightmare—but we don't care. Regardless of the exposure levels, we both know this photo is special: the end of something for us, the beginning of something for them.

The photo op over, Josh and I lift the bike mill up and carry it back to the spot under the tree, carefully placing it in the same ruts it made in the sand when I first climbed on. Josh slaps my back—"We did it, bro!"—and walks over to the truck to start packing up.

I stand silent in front of the bike mill, wondering how to say goodbye. I take a moment to admire it, by far the strongest one I've ever seen, well suited to carry out the work ahead of it. I run my fingers along the handlebars, the slight swoop down, the black plastic grips. My eyes sweep over the green bars to the silver sprocket, following the chain diagonally up to the flywheel, finally settling on the shining white mill, perched there as if on a pedestal. This was the very first grain mill I ever owned, the mill that technically started the Flour Peddler business. Now, it was starting a new journey by returning to its roots. No longer a catchy marketing strategy, a performance piece or an educational tool, it was transitioning back to what it had always been about: grinding on a human scale.

I take a step back, turn around and walk towards the truck. Josh is already inside, and the women are piling in. "Come on, Chris," William calls from the driver's side window. "We are giving everyone who can fit in my truck a ride up to the road at Marial Bai."

I climb into the bed of the truck and sit with my back to the cab window, the women settling around me. As we pull away and start bouncing back on the track through the bush towards Marial Bai, I watch the bike mill get smaller and smaller. Then, at some point, I can't see it anymore. Whether this is because of the dust in the air or the slight moistness in my eyes, I can't tell.

Farewell, Flour Peddler.

13

Exit

Soldiers with machine guns block the doors. December 19, 2013. Hundreds of people crowd around the doors of the Juba International Airport, luggage balanced on heads, stepping over each other and pushing forward. Josh and I embrace before I attempt to enter the scrum. I tell him to go, say I'll be fine, but I know he won't leave until I'm inside the airport.

Trouble is, I can't get inside. There are too many people, and hardly anyone from outside the gate is getting through those double glass doors. Soldiers occasionally open the doors, letting a few people in, even though the crowd inside is nearly spilling out the doorway. Meanwhile, more people arrive and start pushing. As people surge around me, I start to feel claustrophobic and realize I don't want to get stuck in this mass—and for what? Clearly this isn't going to work.

Josh has a better plan. He takes my backpack and tells me to climb over the metal barrier that separates the crowd from the soldiers stationed at the entry. That way, I can cut to the front of the line. He will then heave my backpack over once I'm on the other side, he says.

I can't believe I'm even considering this. A soldier watches me as I scramble up onto a garbage can and find my balance. Josh calls out loudly, "Brother, I'm sure you'll make your flight," less as a reassurance than as a way to broadcast my predicament and show the solider I am a legitimate passenger, and that Josh and I are family.

I hop down on the other side of the barrier, a few inches from the barrel of a machine gun. I squeak out a hello and offer up our final pack of bribery Marlboro cigarettes as Josh heaves over my backpack. The soldier shakes his head and then, sensing my desperation, waves me through.

It's jam-packed inside, but at least everyone has a destination they are moving towards. After nearly two hours of fighting my way forward and dragging my backpack along the floor, I arrive at the Air Uganda check-in counter. My e-ticket says 9:30 a.m. departure. I start to explain my situation—I was stuck outside, along with other Air Uganda customers, I might add—but she waves me off. There's a three-day backlog since the airport was closed, she explains, and Air Uganda would be pleased to put my name on a manifest for a flight leaving at 3:30 p.m. that afternoon. I tell her I'm pleased to hear that. Actually, I'm overjoyed, and as I slouch against the waiting room wall and settle in, I feel my inner cheerleader coming on. I actually did it! I'm going home.

Just like how the flight back to Juba from Aweil worked out yesterday—against the odds.

The hot wind that swept across the Aweil airstrip was like the blast from a hair dryer, so we sat on blue plastic chairs inside a shelter made of woven grass and waited for the plane that would take us to Juba.

This flight was my best shot at getting to Kamloops in time for Christmas. The UN chopper was overbooked, and there was no way Josh and I would get priority over any of the official workers. Besides, thanks to our insistence on having a rock-solid backup plan, we were holding two tickets on Kush Air Flight 122, scheduled to depart from Aweil for Juba that afternoon.

A company whose motto is "Your Satisfaction Is Our Satisfaction," Kush Air is one of several South Sudanese airlines that sprang up after independence in 2011. And while the name may elicit giggles in BC ("Kush" being a term more closely associated with high-potency marijuana production), in South Sudan, Kush Air is a widely recognized brand name, considered the country's leading domestic airline. Actually, it's pretty much the country's only domestic airline, due to the widespread collapse of the competition in the turbulent two years since independence. The Southern Star Airlines only lasted two months.

Although the Kush Air commercial fleet doesn't meet IATA safety standards (actually, it hasn't always met South Sudanese safety standards), at this point, I was not picky. All this plane had to do was get us to Juba. If we missed this flight, that meant I missed my flight from Juba to Entebbe the following day, which meant I would likely miss my KLM flight to Amsterdam and then Seattle the day after that. Maybe in retrospect, the time frame was too tight, but there was no other way we could have pulled off this bike-mill project. Besides, who could have predicted that South Sudan's political struggle, now six months in the making, would culminate in violence, right when we chose to visit?

I reminded myself that we had done the best we could. We had made a plan and a back-up plan. That was pretty much all we could do, which meant that now it was up to Kush Air.

"There might be a problem," William told us in the truck on the way to the airstrip. "The airport in Juba has been closed for the last two days, and today is the first day that any planes have been allowed to fly." That meant there were several days' worth of passengers ahead of us.

I felt anxiety welling up inside me, but William put it to rest. "Chris," he told me, "I will make sure you and Josh get on that plane."

While Josh chatted with an American missionary wearing zip-off shorts and Teva sandals in the waiting area, I scanned the skies for a dot, a speck on the horizon. Nothing. I turned to William. "Do you think the plane has left Juba already?" I asked. He nodded. I got up and started walking, trying to keep myself occupied.

Behind the waiting area and among the scrub brush were huts. I watched a woman exit a low doorway of one and squat down in front of a fire ring, poking the embers under her cooking pot. There were dozens of other huts like this, scattered around the airfield, with women squatting, working and tending to home and family. They probably watch these planes land and take off as if they are from another world, I thought.

Josh poked his head around the corner. "Chris, you're going to want to see this."

I hurried back. Josh pointed off in the distance, where I saw dust clouds rising and the South Sudanese flag flapping. It took me a moment to realize what was happening. The flag was flying from an open-backed military troop transport vehicle, and as it got closer, I saw it was carrying dozens of soldiers, guns pointed upward. The truck was flanked by Jeeps and Land Cruisers driven by men in military uniforms.

I looked over at Josh. "As if it wasn't complicated enough," he said. I looked over at William. When William caught my eye, he smiled and gave me a look like nothing was wrong. But in the second before he noticed me, I saw the truth: he was worried.

The truck skidded to a stop across from the waiting area under a large tree. The soldiers threw their bags on the ground and jumped out, shouting as their boots hit the dirt. They were boisterous, loud, aggressive. A few started moving into formation, but others jostled and jockeyed for position. There was a pushy bounce in their step, a swagger in their stride—the energy men display when they are anticipating a battle.

I turned to Josh. "No photos, okay?" I say. He laughed, and told me not to worry.

William suggested we go drink coffee. He walked away from the waiting area towards one of the huts behind, where an old man was stirring a burbling pot. William ordered three coffees. I tried to sip it slowly, but the thick syrupy taste clogged my throat, leaving me smacking my lips for water.

Another dust cloud, another personnel carrier arrived, and soon there was a full military brigade on display. One man called out, and the others chanted back in unison. Josh asked William why they were here. "Probably waiting to be dispatched," came the detached response. William didn't seem interested in discussing military affairs, and Josh got the point and stopped asking. Then William stood up. "Let's head out of here for a while," he said, walking towards his pickup truck. "Best to avoid these soldiers. You never know what can happen when you have so many guns, and so little training."

We drove slowly along the roads around the airstrip, with no other purpose than just to be somewhere else. We stopped at a construction site, where William got out and chatted with the builders. Josh and I made half-hearted conversation, then I climbed back into the truck and closed my eyes to wait.

Suddenly, I heard a whoosh of air, the sound of engines thrusting into reverse. The black fin of a plane was moving along the runway. Josh and William climbed back into the truck. My heart was in my throat for the entire drive back. What if they board without us? We pulled up and got out. The passengers had already unloaded and were walking past us as we approached the edge of the airstrip. The plane's dual propellers were spinning, and it was loud, dusty and confusing. Do we have to check our tickets with someone?

I turned to William, who acknowledged a high-ranking soldier and then directed us to go towards the open doors. I glanced around. It was not clear who was supposed to go or when. I didn't want to go first, didn't want to be seen as a foreigner asking for preferential treatment, but William slapped my shoulder and said it was okay. "Make it home to your family for Christmas. We'll meet up again, in Vancouver."

Josh and I started walking towards the plane that would take us to Juba. I turned to see William, waving us onward.

"See you again," I said quietly, my voice cracking.

A baby wails. A mother bounces to shush her tired child. A man next to me shouts into his cellphone.

I check the time: 2:30 p.m. Earlier today, passengers were coming and going through the waiting area: RwandAir, now boarding. Kenya Airways, now boarding. But then it just stopped. No passengers departed, and new ones kept arriving, filling the holding area beyond capacity. People sitting, standing, leaning, pushing past other people, threading their way through bodies. Every square centimetre of floor space has been claimed. I've got a wall to lean against, which is good, but I probably couldn't move from this space even if I wanted to.

I want to leave so badly now, to get out, to make it home for Christmas. I've come so far, too far, not to make it now. Please...

My mouth is dry, but there is no water anywhere. The one small kiosk inside the gate has long since sold out, and while there might be some at another kiosk in the main terminal, I'm not about to risk leaving this room and having to re-enter through security. Besides, I have no South Sudanese money left, having used my last forty pounds to pay the official at passport control. "No police registration," he had said, and refused to stamp my passport unless I settled what he claimed I owed. Now all I had left in my money belt were US one-hundred-dollar bills. I start fantasizing about how good it would feel to slap those one-hundred-dollar bills down on a counter to score me a seat on the next plane out. I don't care where it's going or where I end up—Nairobi, Kigali, Addis Ababa, Bujumbura—just get me the hell out of here.

A rumour spreads through the crowd: a plane has crash-landed on the runway! No one can confirm this, but it's clear to everyone that something has gone wrong. The Fly Dubai passengers were supposed to leave at noon, but are still here. Then the story expands: the Fly Dubai plane hit a pothole in the runway and its landing gear crumpled. Not a crash, per se, but it means the runway is blocked, and that means no planes can take off, or land.

Some Kenyan Airways passengers claim to have more information. There is a maintenance crew coming to remove the crippled aircraft, they've heard. Once that happens, we will all be on our way. It's so surreal—a plane crumpled on the runway, today of all days—but I don't know what else to do but get caught up in it. Who cares if it's true? At least there is solidarity in the room.

A man wearing a shirt with a UN insignia on it taps my shoulder. "How're you doing?" he asks. I tell him I'm thirsty but okay. He buys two Red Bulls from the kiosk. "Warm as piss," he says, handing me one. He's taking this all in stride. "Going to Burundi," he says. I nod, but say nothing. "To visit my girlfriend." I smile and tell him I'd rather be with my woman as well.

At 4:30 p.m., the news spreads: the Fly Dubai plane has been cleared from the runway! Someone else has heard from someone else outside the airport, someone who says they saw military planes landing and taking off, evacuating foreigners. That must mean the runway is operating, which means we should be on our way soon. I can feel the mood in the room lift. I start imagining my Ugandan arrival: land in Entebbe, jump in a taxi to Hotel Backpackers, eat a wood-fired pizza and drink some ice-cold Bells. Have a shower, a bowel movement, a long sleep.

At precisely 5:30 p.m., a lady climbs onto a desk in the waiting room and stands up. The noise from the crowd subsides.

"Passengers for Air Uganda," she says loudly. "Your flight is cancelled."

Cancelled? I slump to the floor.

"Come back tomorrow morning," she adds, but no one is listening. People start complaining, arguing: Why can't the planes leave? The runway is clear, correct? What's the problem?

It's going to be dark soon, she says, and there are no runway lights at the Juba International Airport. Once the sun goes down, everything is grounded until sunrise the next morning. She confirms the Kenyan Airways flight did leave Nairobi, but it had to turn back. The Air Uganda flight never left Entebbe.

I don't know what to do. I stay seated on the floor as people pour out of the room. Eight hours in this shithole airport, and now I don't get to leave? There's no way I'm going to make it home in time. How will I tell Amanda-Rae?

I stumble out of the airport feeling utterly defeated. Then I see Josh standing on the walkway, wearing his backpack, waiting for me. "I wasn't going to leave until I saw your plane take off," he says as I run towards him. "I watched the runway, and when I didn't see Air Uganda land, I knew you were stuck."

I don't think I've ever been happier to see my brother. We embrace, then turn around and assess the situation. My backpack is inside the loading zone, and I'm told that retrieving it would bump me off the manifest. Josh and I consider an alternative exit strategy: hire a taxi to drive us two hundred kilometres south to Nimule, where we can cross the border to Uganda, then hop another bus of the Baby Coach variety and attempt to make it back to Kampala in time for my KLM flight to Amsterdam. But we conclude there isn't enough time to go overland. I have to fly.

Josh heads over to the kiosk where we exchanged one hundred

US dollars after we arrived yesterday from Aweil. He got 440 pounds, which we used to pay for hotel rooms, roast chicken sandwiches and motorcycle taxis to the airport early this morning. The shopkeeper takes the one-hundred-dollar bill from Josh and hands back four hundred pounds. Josh says he remembers getting a better exchange rate yesterday. The shopkeeper shrugs.

A soldier barks at us, gun in hand. "The curfew is in effect!" he says. "Go to where you must go." We walk down the road leading away from the airport, but we can't find any motorcycle taxis. We walk farther, still without luck, while the last light leaves the sky. There is no colour left, only the pale blue that comes before black sets in.

As we pass the Tong Ping high-rises, a motorcycle taxi rolls up beside us. We tell him we want him, plus one more motorcycle. He understands and flags another down. Josh and I hop on and head for the office of the Danish Refugee Council.

Josh had been scheduled to work with them after I'd left, documenting their humanitarian assistance programs at the Yida refugee camp in the north of the country, but his assignment was cancelled once the violence broke out and the NGO started evacuating their staff. Earlier today Josh called one of the staff members, who offered him the chance to stay at the compound overnight.

We breeze through the emptying streets, soldiers with guns on every corner. We arrive at the gates of the Danish Refugee Council and shake Julius's hand; he apologizes in advance for not being polite. "I've got a whole load of things to work out," he says, "so you'll need to fend for yourselves. It looks like the shit is about to hit the fan, and I'm in charge of protecting the staff and the compound."

We thank him and agree to stay out of the way. Josh and I sit on the porch of the sleeping quarters and crack open the bottle of Black Label whiskey he had been saving to share with workers in the Yida camp.

"Rebels have taken Bor, less than one hundred miles from us," I overhear Julius talking on Skype, "and we think it's only a matter of time before they hit Juba. The US Department of State is warning of small-arms fire and rocket-propelled grenades by the weekend."

Although Julius doesn't say it, I can tell he is stressed out about us being here. We are just one more thing to deal with, an extra responsibility he didn't sign up for. Josh and I devise a plan to leave for the airport as soon as the morning curfew is lifted. At the airport, I'll try to get inside while Josh waits for the Canadian Embassy representative in the parking lot to register us both for a possible evacuation flight. If my Air Uganda flight departs, I will call Josh and he will get himself out. If my flight doesn't leave, at least I will be on the Canadian list and we can evacuate together.

"That's fine," Julius answers when we tell him the plan. "You can ride to the airport tomorrow with our driver. We're pulling all staff from field offices around the country, so our driver will have to go to the airport anyway to pick them up." Josh and I thank him. "Good, sorted," Julius concludes, and he heads off to his next task.

Josh pours a generous glug of whiskey into his mug, then holds the bottle poised over mine. I wave him off—"I'm feeling queasy already," I say—and he shrugs, sets the bottle down and raises the drink to his lips, wincing as he downs the warm liquor. He raises his eyebrows and reaches over to pour another.

For some reason, his behaviour right now rubs me the wrong way. This hard drinking in the midst of imminent danger, hitting the bottle while gunfire crackles in the distance, this gritty male response—so classic, so romanticized—feels cliché. "You sure fit the whiskey-guzzling foreign correspondent profile," I say to him half-jokingly, which breaks the tension. He smiles and cracks open his laptop, mumbling, "Let's see what the Department of State is advising."

I wander into the kitchen and greet one of the remaining staff members, who is stirring a chicken curry. Sensing my vague, foraging behaviour, he offers me some food. "There's plenty here," he says. "I usually make enough for everyone, but as you can see, there's just a few of us left now."

I nod slowly. He serves me up a heaping portion, the steam rising from the rich brown sauce flowing over the bed of rice. I carry the plate to the table, gazing at the food like it's a mirage. It's been weeks since I've sat in front of anything that looks so appetizing, and my mind spins with anticipation, but my body won't co-operate. My gut is churning, and I have to force myself to take the first bite. The spicy flavours bursting and popping, normally such an integral part of the food experience for me, now evokes the opposite reaction. I swallow hard but press on, telling myself it might be the last meal for a while. "This is really great," I say.

I finish the majority of food on the plate, put my fork down and lean back in the chair. My head is pounding, so I grab a bottle of Tylenol from my bag and head outside into the compound, where I find Josh sitting with the whiskey bottle. I sit down and we are quiet, listening to the sounds of shots being fired under sparkling stars.

We both awake long before dawn. I give Julius a groggy "good morning," take a swig of water, and busy myself packing and re-packing my bag. We load everything into the Land Cruiser that is idling inside the compound gates as the minutes tick down to the end of curfew. Then we hit the road.

Three hours later, my Air Uganda flight lifts off into the sky. On the flight I insist on coffee, even though they are only offering tea. I finally relent, load up the tea with Coffee-Mate and sugar and then set to work filling out the Ugandan customs entry card. It's only then that I realize today is December 20: the day before the winter solstice. My thoughts drift back to Roberts Creek and the community feast that will be held to mark the transition of the seasons, from the longest night of the year onward to longer days. From darkness to light.

Soon after I finish the landing card, we begin our descent into Entebbe, where Josh and I had arrived eleven days earlier. Just like I'd planned yesterday, I jump in the first available taxi and head to the Hotel Backpackers where we spent our first night. It is only 11:00 a.m., but I order a beer, then a hamburger, then another beer. As the backpackers rouse from their slumber and order breakfasts, trading tales of river rafting and waterfall swimming, I reflect on my experiences.

I think about all the people still stranded at the Juba airport. I think about the twenty thousand people seeking refuge in UN compounds around Juba, and the tens of thousands of others at UN bases across the country. I think about the progress South Sudan had made since independence and the struggles that lie ahead.

"Hey, mate!" An Aussie backpacker with flowing blond hair slaps my back. "Been up to much in Uganda?"

I shake my head. "Just arrived," I say.

"You'll love it, mate," he says, tucking into his pancakes and fruit. "Loads of hippos, crocs—and loads of girls, hey?"

I polish off the last swig of beer and head to my hostel bed, where I crash out for several hours. When I open my laptop that evening, I see a message from Dad in my inbox: JOSH IS SAFE IN ADDIS ABABA. Turns out Josh called Dad half an hour ago from onboard a Dutch military evacuation flight heading to Ethiopia.

I use the news about Josh as a pretext to celebrate, and I spend the night drinking cheap whiskey and dancing to bass-heavy reggae in Kampala's flashy nightclubs. I have only a vague recollection of the motorcycle taxi that brought me back to my bed at 4:00 a.m. I wake to a monster of a hangover, and spend a queasy day on the shores of Lake Victoria while I wait to check in for my KLM flight to Amsterdam.

Paper stars, snowflakes and glossy red bells dangle from the rafters of the Starbucks inside Schiphol Amsterdam Airport. The layover is short, and the connecting flight to Seattle is a blur: seat buckles, safety instructions, bad movies and fitful naps. In Seattle I collect my bag, stained red by the African dust, and take a cab to the hotel where Josh and I left the car with our winter coats inside. The damp cold of the Pacific Northwest chills me to the bone, and I'm shivering as I climb in and blast the heat. The windshield wipers slash along Interstate 5 north to the border, where the South Sudanese visa in my passport provides cause to search the vehicle. Two hours later, I arrive at Josh's house in East Vancouver, where Mom and Dad greet me with hugs and tears.

Early the next morning, Dad drives me across the Arthur Laing Bridge to the Vancouver International Airport, where I board a small plane bound for Kamloops. An hour later, ice crunching underfoot, I walk out the automatic doors of the airport and embrace my family—in time for Christmas. The next three days are a montage of holiday songs, kids running wild, rich food and milky eggnog. When I arrive back on the Sunshine Coast five days later, I see that Dad has turned the grain shack into a tool shed.

Like a recovering alcoholic who now sees the life he nearly drank away, I view everything with fresh eyes. I breathe in the ocean air, strain to hear the cries of seagulls. I realize how much I've missed the crashing waves, so Amanda-Rae and I pile the kids into the car and drive to the Roberts Creek beach. As the kids clamber out, I look at the back seat and notice there is no flour dust anywhere.

My phone vibrates, but I don't want to answer it. I want this moment to be pristine, free from digital interruptions. I want to enjoy my family, not be tethered to technology. The trip to East Africa purged me of the need to be constantly connected, and I want to see how long I can hold that feeling. I'm a guy that has always had multiple things on the go, but for that short time with Josh, the purpose was singular: build the bike mill. Now, we can both move on.

I watch the waves foaming as they crash against the rocks. My phone vibrates again. I give up and check it. It's a message from Josh: Chapter One done!

I click the phone off and look at Amanda-Rae, who smiles softly and embraces me. Solomon and Gretchen crowd around, hugging my legs, shouting, "Dad, watch this!" and "Dad, check this out!"

The Flour Peddler hasn't ended; it has been transformed. We left the bike mill in a remote region of the world's youngest country, on the other side of the planet from where it began, where it can serve the most fundamental purpose of all: supporting local food.

Whatever happens next, I'm sure of one thing: we've got quite a story to share.

Epilogue

The line crackles, then connects. "Josh," I start in quickly, "there's a problem with the grinder!"

It's September 26, 2014, 2:14 p.m. Haitian time. I'm calling Josh from a small village ninety kilometres from Port au Prince, using a newly purchased cellphone, which I hope has enough minutes on it to call Canada. The closest place to get more minutes is a wooden kiosk out at the road junction, half a kilometre away. With the time zone lag, it is not yet noon back in Vancouver, and Josh would normally be prepping for his weekly lecture at the Boucher Institute of Naturopathic Medicine, where he and I co-teach a research methodology course.

"Do you have the number for the Country Living rep?" I blurt out, not wanting to waste time.

"What's up?" he asks.

"The auger won't spin when there's grain in it," I explain. "It works fine when it's empty, but it won't feed the corn through to the grinding plates. It was golden at the metal workshop yesterday, so I don't know what happened. Anyway, I need to call Joel and ask him for advice."

"Okay," Josh replies, sensing the urgency in my voice. He does a quick web search, then says, "I'll text the number to your phone, but here it is: Three, six, zero …"

I grab a broken stick and scrawl the ten digits in the dirt between the roots of a tall mango tree. "Good luck?" he offers. Then the line clicks.

This bike mill was supposed to be easy. Or at least easier than it was in South Sudan. Even before I left, I had a contact on the ground in Haiti—Israel Louis, the contact for my PhD fieldwork study, which focuses on a range of supply chain dynamics between small-holder mango farmers in Haiti's Plateau Central region and international markets and organizations. I had secured a generous donation from the Sechelt Rotary Club. The bike-mill construction had gone off without a hitch.

Now, a problem with the internal components of the mill itself could ruin everything. I hadn't anticipated the mill being stuck in the rain.

I look over at the bike mill, painted bright red. Just before it arrived, I imagined the sweet taste of victory: children squealing, women smiling and men laughing as ground corn flowed from the mill. I would show them how to take it apart and clean it, how to adjust the grind, talk about how it would last a long time if cared for properly.

But once it arrived, I could see right away there was a problem: the grinding plates were stuck. I squatted down to the level of the grinding knob and tried to crank it open, but it wouldn't budge.

"Ce ne peux pas ouvre," I say over my shoulder, as I continue trying to spin the knob loose. I feel frustration mounting as it refuses to move. What I wouldn't give to hear that loud grinding sound now. My anxiety level rising, I try to explain the situation, but I'm struggling to remember the French word for "stuck," so I default to the high school textbook style: *"C'est ferme...et ce n'est pas bon."*

"Not good." Now that's an understatement.

Three days earlier, I had paid seven thousand gourdes—$180 US—to the welders at the outdoor welding shop in Petit Rivière de l'Artibonite to design and build a bike mill. The price included delivery to the village of Hatte Jumelle, seven kilometres away, where I was doing my PhD research. No problem, the owner of the shop had assured me; there is a pickup truck that transports goods to that village every so often. As soon as the bike mill was completed, he had told me, it would be shipped out: *"Plus rapide, et pas de problème."*

Since the experience in South Sudan, I now know the design and how to implement it. Cut several lengths of metal, weld them into boxes, and then weld those into a three-dimensional cube. Add a crossbar through the middle with a pedal mechanism set inside it, a seat and handlebars. Weld a solid metal plate at the front where the grinder will sit and a sprocket to the flywheel of the mill. Bolt the grinder on, string a chain between the flywheel and the pedals, and voila! Bike mill number two, locked and loaded, ready for delivery.

There was just one small problem, the owner of the shop said as I readied the bike mill for departure. The pickup truck was no longer going to Hatte Jumelle. Maybe some other truck near the market would be going in a few days' time, he offered.

It hit me like a ton of bricks. I was leaving the country in a few days, and I had to get back to Hatte Jumelle for a series of meetings before I departed. I didn't have time to wait.

I decided to take matters into my own hands. Israel called Yvannel, my trusty chauffeur, who I've relied on to transport me along the bone-shattering roads of rural Haiti on the back of his motorcycle since I started my PhD research.

Yvannel pulled up to the shop, saw the bike mill and laughed. I knew he was thinking, Chris, you cannot sit on the back of my motorcycle holding that. It is probably one hundred pounds! I doubted he could even make it happen, but he felt confident it would work. "We will get it there," he said. "But first, I will take you back to Hatte Jumelle in time for your meeting."

The clouds were gathering, so Yvannel drove faster than usual. In the seven kilometres, I didn't see any other vehicles getting through the lingering sticky mud from yesterday's rain, only motorcycles and donkeys.

Maybe this bike mill will have to go by donkey, in the end…

Half an hour later, Yvannel dropped me at the field site, and then turned to go. "I'll get your pedal machine here tonight, I promise," he said. I clasped his hand, told him I believed him and watched him slip and slide back down the road until he was out of sight.

I went back to my room and it wasn't too long before the downpour started. It rattled the tin roof, the pools of mud swelling below with each passing minute.

The bike mill didn't arrive that evening as scheduled. The next afternoon, when it finally rolled into the village, carried by a strong passenger on the back of Yvannel's motorcycle, I was overjoyed. But as Yvannel explained their struggle—they had started out for Hatte Jumelle as soon as they could, but a torrential rain shower forced then to turn back after twenty minutes—I started getting anxious.

The rain. Oh no! The mill!

The downpour I had heard yesterday—the rain that had forced them to turn back—had soaked the bike mill. I looked at the grinding mechanism, still glistening with moisture from the previous day's downpour. It had sat in the shop for more than eighteen hours, trickles of rainwater penetrating the interior—all the mechanical parts that the manual says need to stay dry.

"*C'est coincée.*" It's jammed, one man says.

"*Oui,*" I reply, and tell them there is water inside.

Hearing that it was stuck, a few men step forward, offering muscle power. They grunt and try to turn the wheel. I use this distraction to escape. I don't want the local children to see me lose it, so I walk behind the brick outhouse, where I let out a scream. Then I start back, ready to face the challenge.

Nearly an hour passes. The novelty of watching me struggle, curse, stride away and return having finally worn off, the crowd has thinned, but not dissipated. By now, my hands are raw from trying to turn the knob.

Finally, after pouring cooking oil through the mechanism as a lubricant, I manage to hammer the knob open, forcing the grinding plates apart. I'm dripping with sweat and my hands are greasy, but the mill spins. I break out in a smile.

Some people start clapping. Now, the moment of truth: I pour in the corn and tell the anxious kid sitting on the seat to start pedalling. The mill spins freely now, but the corn doesn't move.

I look over at the phone number for Country Living Grain Mills scratched in the dirt. "Try bending that spring inside," Joel tells me over the phone. "Yep, to the left. Or to the right. And make sure the little key is nice and solid."

The key? Where is that? I look in the space where the key should be, but it's MIA. It must have fallen out somewhere along the way. Maybe it's on the floor of the shop? Maybe it fell out during the motorcycle ride? Where to even begin?

Some people might admit defeat at this point, but not me. I push the corn through with my fingers, turn the crank, and a few flakes of cornmeal spill out. I empty it and try again, watching the auger spin perfectly when empty, but remain still when the corn is inside. Having triumphed over the challenge of the rusty plates, I'm now stymied by a key smaller than my baby finger.

Israel pats me on the back and smiles. He can see I'm disheartened. "I'm sorry," I tell him. "I really wanted to show the people how this pedal mill works, and how much fun it can be to ride the bike and grind your corn. The kids will love it, too." He assures me the auger issue is a small problem that can be easily fixed back at the metal shop. He promises me he will get this up and running. There is no other grinding machine in Hatte Jumelle, he says, let alone something as strong and as well-built as this grinder. He tells me that a long time ago, there used to be a hand mill for people to use, but it broke and was never repaired. This one is strong, he tells me; the people will be happy.

The crowd starts to disperse, with men patting me on the back and children smiling. The people living here are patient. I hoist up the bike mill, carry it inside an army tent in the corner of the yard, which is used to store crates for the upcoming harvest, and cover the grinder with plastic bags to ensure it stays dry. All I can do is hope Israel is right, that soon this bike mill will be spinning, then corn flowing. In fact, I know it will work, I tell myself. I trust him.

It's been a year and a half since I sold my last bag of flour, and I don't miss it. That might seem strange after the many years I spent as an integral link in southwestern BC's grain chain. But that was then, and this is now. As Josh and I discussed in South Sudan, once we wrote the book, the Flour Peddler would be in the past tense.

But I don't want to stop building bike mills. Especially after constructing this second bike mill, despite its trials and tribulations, I'm hooked on the rush of it. This endeavour, which Josh and I call Continuous Cycle Enterprises, is still a milling enterprise, but it's about other people's milling, about food processing in remote locations where few alternatives exist. Places where it's "handcrafted" by default.

For five years, my bike mills were teaching tools and marketing gimmicks, not agricultural machines. The Flour Peddler was always about the concept, not the execution. But now, the purpose has been transformed. It's no longer an educational and performance tool designed to teach kids and adults the value of fresh flour and the role of the small-scale miller in a large-scale world. Now, it's about increasing food processing capacity in a way that supports local food.

Despite this change in direction, the underlying purpose is the same: building relationships. Relationships with donors and partners, with welders and engineers, with motorcycle or truck drivers, and with people where the bike mill is constructed, as well as the end users at its final destination.

We aren't idealists. We don't think that quick impact, low-tech agriculture machines can save the world. But they might just save someone some time and energy, as well as give that person the capacity to start a micro-enterprise. Besides, building bike mills (or fruit slicers or grain threshers) in off-grid locations around the world is guaranteed to be full of adventure and unknowns—something that has drawn Josh and me together for longer than we can remember.

Merging these three principles—supporting local food processing capacity, building relationships and creating adventure—has resulted in a new business that, as Thiessen would rightly tell us, runs counter to the very logic of capitalism.

But perhaps it follows the logic of a new kind of capitalism, one that doesn't result in any ROI for the initial investor, but stimulates the economy in the destination country. Sure, we could mass-produce these bike mills in China and ship them to rural locations around the world, but that would miss the point. Instead, we want to work with people on the ground, at every stage of the process.

The formula is simple: travel with a Country Living Grain Mill and let the local economy take care of the rest. Purchase the basic parts at a local bicycle shop, hire local engineers to design it, local metalworkers to fabricate it and local truck drivers to transport it to its destination. The result will be a bike mill suitable for the local conditions, and several new relationships with people along the way.

Panlang, South Sudan. Hatte Jumelle, Haiti. Where are we going next?

Find out how you can participate in our bike-mill revolution at www.continuouscycle.ca.

Chris exploring the settlements around Aweil.

South Sudan Update

As this book went to press, the conflict in South Sudan that began on December 15, 2013, has resulted in thousands of deaths, and forced hundreds of thousands of people to flee their homes for the safety of UN compounds inside the country and refugee camps on the Ethiopian border. While initial news reports of the violence perpetrated is horrific in and of itself—stories of people being dragged from hospital beds into the street and shot, towns and villages looted and burned to the ground—the continued effects of this massive population displacement that followed have been just as deadly. The summer rains, life-giving in times of stability, have instead wreaked havoc, cutting off emergency aid workers and flooding refugee camps and UN bases that are filled with internally displaced people. Disease has run rampant, and thousands more innocent people have died.

The long-term effects of the conflict are just as insidious. Displaced people cannot tend their fields or farms, and having missed an entire cycle of planting and harvesting, the spectre of famine now looms large for them. World Food Programme figures suggest that nearly four million South Sudanese—out of a total population of eight million—now face the prospect of starvation.

It has been heartbreaking to watch from the safety and comfort of our living rooms as the world's youngest country spirals downward. Over the past twelve months, several promising ceasefire agreements have been signed, and then dashed as warring parties violate the newly inked treaties, each side accusing the other of instigating violence and carrying out atrocities.

At times like these, we try to remain positive. We think back to William's urban farm, remembering the bounty spread out before us as we walked along the burbling irrigation channels that watered the fields. We remember the wide smiles from farmers who pulled giant tubers from the moist soil in the middle of the dry season, while the surrounding landscape cracked in the sun.

We don't believe one man's work can save an entire country. But we believe that William's work with the Pan Aweil Development Agency offers a vision of food security in a place where, with boreholes and treadle pumps, crops can be planted and harvested year-round. Where context-appropriate development can feed the local community and nurture budding entrepreneurs at the same time.

As we walked through the fields, William had told us, "Before I started, people didn't believe you could grow food here during the dry season. So I told them, you have the sun already. Let Pan Aweil help you get the water. The rest is up to you."

To find out more about the Pan Aweil Development Agency, visit www.panaweil.net.

Following pages: The Aweil urban farm was started by William Kolong, and is tended by the local villagers.

Page 246: A man enters his compound in Terekeka, South Sudan.

Page 250: A boy in Terekeka, South Sudan, holds his baby brother.

Acknowledgements

This book would not have been possible without the tireless and unwavering support from our parents. So Mom and Dad—you deserve all the glory.

To the team at Caitlin Press, Vici, Andrea and Ben—thanks for your faith in us and our book, and your extra efforts to help us through the process.

To William Kolong and the Pan Aweil Development Agency—you are an inspiration, and the work you do is clearly making a difference in the lives of the people in your homeland.

To Christopher Douglas and Lone Star Africa Works—thanks for your support, assistance and advice. We look forward to future collaborations.

To Christopher and the gang at the Juba Technical Secondary School—thanks to you, we have a robust mill and a model for future small-scale agricultural machines.

To Joel Jenkins at Country Living Grain Mills—thanks for hooking us up with the strongest and most bombproof mill on the planet, and for your continued contributions to our overseas adventures.

To John Thiessen at Vertex One Asset Management and Randy Shore at the *Vancouver Sun*—thanks for helping us get this project noticed.

To the contributors to our crowdfunding campaign and all the supporters and customers who bought flour from us over the years—we salute and thank you for your commitment to the cause of fresh flour and local food processors.

Specific Thanks from Chris Hergesheimer

To my wife, Amanda-Rae, and my children, Solomon and Gretchen—I couldn't have done any of this without your support and love. You are my family muse—*muchas gracias.*

To my brother and co-author of this crazy adventure—you are truly a gifted writer. Thanks for all your work in translating my years of experiences into this epic tale. Here's to future adventures and hopefully the documentation of those. And to my sister-in-law, Holly—thank you for your late-night red-pen copyediting of early versions of this manuscript.

To Hannah Wittman, my postgraduate supervisor—I wouldn't have started this without you, and I look forward to our work together over the coming years.

To the whole gang at FarmFolk CityFolk—you introduced me to a world full of questions about the value of a sustainable food system. I have enjoyed every minute of it.

To all the farmers, millers, bakers, activists and educators in southwestern BC who assisted with my MA thesis research—you've inspired me, justified the existence of the Flour Peddler and given me hope for the future.

Specific Thanks from Josh Hergesheimer

To Chris, my brother, intellectual compatriot and travel companion—I could not have written this story without you. Thanks for your contributions, your input and your trust in me that the book would turn out as amazing as I promised.

To Holly, my wife and manuscript editor—I loved watching you pore over the words, shaping the paragraphs, refining the phrasing and suggesting structural changes that made the story shine.

To all the Dutch embassy staff and the Royal Netherlands Air Force involved in the military evacuation flight from Juba on December 20, 2013—thanks for your professionalism and your willingness to assist Canadians and welcome them onboard your aircraft. You did your country proud.

To J.B. MacKinnon and Robin Esrock—thanks for reading our book and spreading the word. With your support, we've found the "local food, global adventure travel" niche.

To Daniel Wood, my writing instructor—thanks for your constant reminders about the narrative arc. I now draw story caterpillars at 3:00 a.m. to stay on track.

To Ross Howard, Frances Bula, Nick Read, Les Bazso, Robert Dykstra, Ann Roberts, Kathryn Gretsinger, Effie Klein and Gene Keith from the Langara College Journalism Department—thanks for training me to write clearly and concisely while I tried to parent twin infants and meet assignment deadlines.

To ambient electronic artists Carbon Based Lifeforms and Stellardrone—thanks for providing such inspiring music, the perfect soundtrack for writing this book.

Bibliography

Antle, J.M., and V.H. Smith, eds. *The Economics of World Wheat Markets*. UK & New York: CABI Publishing, 1999.

BC Ministry of Agriculture. Second Report to the Ministry of Agriculture. Ottawa: Ministry of Agriculture, 1893.

BC Ministry of Agriculture and Lands. Regional Profile: Lower Mainland. 2002. Retrieved March 8, 2008, from www.agf.gov.bc.ca/stats/regional/mainland.htm.

Born, Branden, and Mark Purcell. "Avoiding the local trap scale and food systems in planning research."*Journal of Planning Education and Research* 26, no. 2 (2006): 195–207. Accessed July 12, 2007. http://www.agroecology.wisc.edu/courses/agroecology-702/materials/9-farm-and-comm-viability/born-purcell-2006.pdf.

Carr, Mike. *Bioregionalism and Civil Society: Democratic Challenges to Corporate Globalism*. Vancouver: UBC Press, 2004.

Connell, David J., and Christopher Hergesheimer. "Strengthening the Core Business of Farmers Markets through Strategic Business Planning." *Journal of Agriculture, Food Systems, and Community Development* 4, no. 4 (2014): 97–108. Accessed November 24, 2014. http://www.agdevjournal.com/volume-4-issue-4/475-core-business-farmers-markets.html.

Connell, David J., John Smithers, and Alun Joseph. "Farmers' markets and the 'good food' value chain: a preliminary study." *Local Environment* 13, no. 3 (2008): 169–185. Accessed March 28, 2009. http://www.tandfonline.com.ez-proxy.library.ubc.ca/doi/full/10.1080/13549830701669096.

Deng, Francis Mading. *The Dinka of the Sudan*. Illinois: Waveland Press Inc., 1984.

Eggers, Dave. *What Is the What? The Autobiography of Valentino Achak Deng*. San Francisco: McSweeney's, 2006.

Fitzpatrick, Mary, Anthony Ham, Dean Starnes, and Trent Holden. *East Africa Guidebook*. 9th ed. Franklin: Lonely Planet Publications, 2012.

Fortes, M., and E.E. Evans-Pritchard eds. *The Nuer of the Southern Sudan in African Political Systems*, 272–296. London: Oxford University Press, 1940.

George, Rose. *Ninety Percent of Everything: Inside Shipping, the Invisible Industry That Puts Clothes on Your Back, Gas in Your Car, and Food on Your Plate*. New York: Metropolitan Books, 2013.

Halweil, Brian. "Local Food." World Watch Institute. Accessed October 1, 2014. http://www.worldwatch.org/system/files/local%20Food.pdf.

Hergesheimer, Christopher, and Hannah Wittman. "Weaving chains of grain: Alternative grain networks and social value in British Columbia." *Food, Culture and Society: An Inter-*

national Journal of Multidisciplinary Research 15, no. 3 (2012): 375–393. Accessed August 20, 2012. http://www. ingentaconnect.com.ezproxy.library.ubc.ca/content/blooms-bury/fcs/2012/00000015/00000003/art00003.

Keen, David. *Benefits of Famine: A Political Economy of Famine and Relief in Southwestern Sudan, 1983–1989.* Eastern African Studies. Suffolk, UK: James Currey (imprint of Boydell & Brewer Ltd.), 2008.

Keen, David. *Complex Emergencies.* Cambridge: Polity Press, 2008.

Kunstler, James Howard. *The Long Emergency: Surviving the Converging Catastrophes of the Twenty-first Century.* New York: Grove/Atlantic, 2005.

Lovell-Hoare, Sophie, and Max Lovell-Hoare. *South Sudan.* England: Bradt Travel Guides Ltd., 2013.

Natsios, Andrew S. *Sudan, South Sudan, and Darfur: What Everyone Needs to Know.* Oxford: Oxford University Press, 2012.

Ormsby, Margaret A. "Agricultural Development in British Columbia." *Agricultural History* 19, no. 1 (1945): 11–20. Accessed December 19, 2008. http://www.jstor.org.ezproxy.library.ubc.ca/stable/3739693.

Rosenthal, Elizabeth. "Environmental Cost of Shipping Groceries Around the World." *New York Times*, April 26, 2008. Accessed Feb 29, 2014. http://www.nytimes.com/2008/04/26/business/worldbusiness/26food.html?pagewanted=all&_r=0.

Smith, Anthony D. *Nationalism and Modernism*. London: Routledge, 1998.

Smith, Alisa, and J.B. MacKinnon. *The 100-Mile Diet: A Year of Local Eating*. Toronto: Vintage Canada, 2007.

Thesiger, Wilfred. *The Life of my Choice*. New York: W. W. Norton & Co. Inc. 1980.

Ward, Tony. "The Origins of the Canadian Wheat Boom, 1880–1910." *Canadian Journal of Economics* (1994): 865–83. Accessed January 21, 2009. http://www.jstor.org.ezproxy. library.ubc.ca/stable/136188.

Websites

APHLIS. African Postharvest Losses Information System: A Transnational Network of Cereal Grain Experts. "Loss Tables: Maize, S. Sudan 2003–2013." Accessed September 20, 2014. http://www.aphlis.net/?form=losses_estimates&co_id=44&prov_id=603&c_id=324&year=2013.

Canadian Grain Commission: Exports of Canadian Grain and Wheat Flour. Accessed January 6, 2015. http://www.grainscanada.gc.ca/statistics-statistiques/ecgwf-egcfb/ecgm-megc-eng.htm.

Canadian National Millers Association. Accessed November 1, 2014. http://www.canadianmillers.ca.

Food and Agriculture Organization of the United Nations: Cereal Supply and Demand Brief. Accessed December 12, 2014. http://www.fao.org/worldfoodsituation/csdb/en.

Radio Tamazuj: Sudanese News Crossing Borders. Accessed December 12, 2014. https://radiotamazuj.org.

Sudan Tribune: Plural News and Views on Sudan. http://www.sudantribune.com.

World Food Programme: South Sudan Food Security Situation Overview. Accessed January 6, 2015. https://www.wfp.org/countries/south-sudan/food-security.

PHOTO SAM CHUA

CHRIS HERGESHEIMER (right) is a research, policy and project management consultant on issues surrounding food and farming. Chris has a master of arts in sociology from Simon Fraser University and is a PhD candidate in the department of Land and Food Systems at the University of British Columbia. Chris is also the director of research education at the Boucher Institute of Naturopathic Medicine. He lives in Roberts Creek, BC.

JOSH HERGESHEIMER (left) is a writer and photographer. He has a master of arts in human rights from the University of Sussex and a master of science in nationalism and ethnicity from the London School of Economics. His writing and photography have appeared in the *Vancouver Sun*, the *Vancouver Observer*, *This* magazine, *Al-Jazeera International*, the *Globe & Mail* and the *Georgia Straight*. Since travelling to South Sudan, he was commissioned by the Overseas Press Club of America to write a guide for journalists visiting the country. Josh lives in Vancouver.